# **Blessed Assurance**

## A Defense
of the Doctrine of
Eternal Security

Steven Waterhouse
Th.M., D.Min.

Westcliff Press
P. O. Box 1521, Amarillo, TX 79105

## Suggested Cataloging-in-Publication Data

Waterhouse, Steven W.
    Blessed Assurance; A Defense of the Doctrine of Eternal
Security/Steven W. Waterhouse
    100 p. 18 cm
    Includes Biblical references
    ISBN 0-9702418-1-X
    1. Bible – Theology  2.Theology – Doctrinal 3. Bible –
Research 4. Pastoral theology
    Suggested Library of Congress Number: BS543
    Suggested Dewey Number: 230.041

# About The Author

Dr. Steven W. Waterhouse has served as the Pastor of Westcliff Bible Church in Amarillo, Texas, since 1985. Dr. Waterhouse has degrees from Dallas Theological Seminary (D. Min.); Capital Bible Seminary, Lanham MD (Th.M., Hebrew and Greek); Spring Arbor College, Michigan (B.A., Social Science); and Cornerstone University in Grand Rapids, MI.

This study is an excerpt from a detailed work on systematic theology written by Dr. Waterhouse entitled, *Not By Bread Alone; An Outlined Guide to Bible Doctrine.*

Information about this book and others written by Dr. Waterhouse can be accessed at his web site at:

http://www.webtheology.com

# <u>Other Titles By Steven Waterhouse</u>

*Not By Bread Alone; An Outlined
Guide to Bible Doctrine*

*What Must I Do To Be Saved;
The Bible's Definition of Saving Faith*

*Strength For His People; A Ministry
For the Families of the Mentally Ill*

*The Sanctity of Life*

*Depression; Biblical Causes and Counseling*

*Demons or Mental Illness?*

---

Second Printing 2004

Westcliff Press
P.O. Box 1521
Amarillo TX 79105
1-806-359-6362
westcliff@amaonline.com

ISBN: 0-9702418-1-X
Library of Congress Catalog Card Number 00-134699

Printed in the United States of America

"Scripture taken from the NEW AMERICAN STANDARD BIBLE,
Copyright The Lockman Foundation 1960, 1962, 1963, 1968,
1971, 1972, 1973, 1975, 1977, 1995
"Used by permission". [www.Lockman.org.]
Note: Minor variations exist because the NASB undergoes periodic
refinements. Most quotes are from the 1977 version.

# Dedication

*For my lifelong peers – Gary Allen, Stephen Baird,
Greg Smith, and Ken Wiest – and mentors – Don
Phillips and Bill Waterhouse. You have proven that
distance and time need not diminish friendship
(Proverbs 17:17, 18:24)*

*Steven Waterhouse*

# Acknowledgments

Many faithful servants of God labored
on this project. My own strength
would have failed without you.

Hugh Akin
Dan Bentley
Daphne Cox
Mary Daily
Dwight Davis
Janet Kampschroeder
Gabriel Trevizo
Alan N. Good, Editor

The congregation of Westcliff Bible Church, Amarillo, TX,
deserves praise for allowing pastoral energies to be devoted to
Bible study and for the financial backing of Bible research
projects.

# Blessed
# Assurance

## Table Of Contents

# Blessed Assurance

# Preface

While the conclusion of this book is that the Bible teaches the eternal security of the believer, one can at least understand those who use proof-texts which they think disprove this doctrine. One can even admire those who acknowledge the Bible as their authority—while at the same time questioning the accuracy of their conclusions. What is difficult to understand is the view of some that the issue of eternal security is unimportant. How can a serious Christian not care to search the Scriptures on this vital topic concerning his or her eternal destiny?

Believers who deny eternal security are still believers. Disagreement on this doctrine is not the dividing line between the "sheep and the goats" or the "wheat and the tares." However, the doctrine of eternal security is perhaps the most important doctrine that divides the faithful. A person's view on eternal security determines his total outlook and motivation in Christian living. Every believer must search the Scriptures to find truth in this area. With concern and respect to Bible-believers on both sides of this debate, *Blessed Assurance* is offered with the intent of inspiring everyone to look to the Bible for answers.

# **Blessed Assurance**

*A Defense of the Doctrine of Eternal Security*

Many Christians think Bible doctrine is irrelevant to "real life". On the contrary, what one believes affects how one lives. Though Paul's comments in 2 Thess. 2:2 involve end-time doctrines, the apostle's concern shows the practical impact of errors in doctrine. Because of mistaken doctrine, the Thessalonians were "shaken from composure", "disturbed", "unsettled" (NIV), and "alarmed" (NIV). The wrong conclusion on eternal security can produce the same results in the lives of Christians today. The author has personally counseled people for depression, even to the point of potential suicide, because they had felt they had lost salvation. Even when the results are not such a deep crisis, a person's conclusion on eternal security shapes the entire course of Christian living. Do we dedicate our lives to God in gratitude for His undeserved blessings, or must we labor in fear of missing forgiveness, resurrection, and heaven? Are we blanketed in God's unconditional and changeless love, or are we moving along a thin tightrope with a potential to plunge into hell through failing? Doctrinal issues do matter in real life.

In researching any Bible doctrine, one must give priority to texts that are clear and not subject to alternative interpretations. Then verses that are capable of more than one conclusion should be reconciled to them. In other words, possible interpretations of controversial texts should only be accepted if they are compatible with simple and clear texts. This is the method employed in this study.

We will begin by showing that major and clear doctrines such as salvation by faith, predestination, sealing by the Holy Spirit, etc., support eternal security. Then we will consider numerous texts, which in isolation could teach that believers lose salvation. Yet, these same verses can also be understood in ways that fit the conclusion that salvation is secure. The reader will notice it takes more space to deal with problem passages than to state the case for the believer's eternal security. Do not mistake this for a weak conclusion. Material in support of eternal security can be brief because eternal security is based upon simple and clear Bible truths.

# Evidences for Eternal Security

## If we view the subject from a negative perspective, then:

### If a Christian can lose salvation, then Christ must lose His righteousness

Justification by faith, when correctly understood, supports the eternal security of the believer. When Christ died, our sins were imputed (credited) to **His** account. When a person trusts in Christ, Christ's righteousness is imputed (credited) to the **believer's account.** God views a believer's position as "in Christ" and covered with Christ's righteousness. On this basis, the believer is declared legally just. **It is Christ's righteousness** (not human righteousness and merit) **that is the basis of a believer's acceptance and standing with God**. Self-righteousness did not save in the first place, and it is not a basis upon which salvation is continued. Christ's righteousness brings salvation. So the real issue in a believer's security is not the endurance of human righteousness but the **eternal nature** of Christ's **righteousness**.

A believer cannot lose his righteousness or righteous legal standing before God unless Christ loses His righteousness, and that cannot and will not occur. His righteousness is eternal. Our own human self righteousness is as filthy rags at best and plays no part whatsoever in the gift of salvation (Isa. 64:6).

Christ's righteousness, and Christ's righteousness alone, justifies the person who believes (Rom. 4:5). Relative to justification, God never considered our own righteousness or lack of it, rather He looked to Christ's holy perfect righteousness that has been imputed to (credited to) a believer. (See Rom. 5:17-19; 1 Cor. 1:30; 2 Cor. 5:21, also Eph. 1:6-7; Col. 2:10.) Maintaining that a believer can lose salvation and become unjustified is the same as believing that Christ can lose His righteousness because it is His righteousness that must be lost in order to become "unjustified." A believer cannot lose His justification until Christ loses His righteousness. Even the proposal of the concept is absurd. Christ's death provides salvation, but His life also plays a significant role in the salvation plan. Rom. 5:10 teaches that just as Christ's death saves the believer, so does His life. If trusting in Christ reconciles us to God at a time when we were enemies, how much more secure is the believer's position now that he has been credited with the righteousness of Christ's holy, perfect, sinless life. Paul confidently asserts, "we shall be saved by **His life**." The merits of Christ's holy, perfect, sinless righteous life belong to those with faith. His righteous life will never lose righteousness. Thus, Paul can assert that the future outcome for believers is "we shall be saved," and believers need not worry about the future of their salvation. It is certainly secure.

- For if while we were enemies, we were

reconciled to God through the death of His
Son, much more, having been reconciled,
we shall be saved by **His life** [Rom. 5:10].

• He made Him who knew no sin to be sin on
  our behalf, that we might become the righteousness of God **in Him** [2 Cor. 5:21].

*If a Christian can lose salvation, then God is not
all-powerful, and the Bible is wrong on predestination*

Regardless of whether one views election as con-
ditional or unconditional, all must agree that **God's
program of predestination extends** far beyond the
time of conversion **to future glory in eternity.**

• For whom He foreknew, He also **predestined to become conformed to the image
  of His Son**, that He might be the first-born
  among many brethren; and whom He predestined, these He also called; and whom
  He called, these He also justified; and
  whom He justified, these He also **glorified**
  [Rom. 8:29-30].

Everyone that has been justified (i.e., all believers) is so certain of glorification that glory can be
spoken of in the **past tense**. The believer (justified
one) is predestined to glory by God's decree. The
goal of predestination is a conforming to the image
of God's Son. This will occur at the Rapture. All
those predestined (i.e., all believers) **must** obtain that

point, "When He appears, **we shall be like Him...**"(**1 John 3:2**). In addition, the phrase "predestined us to adoption as sons" in Eph. 1:5 supports a predestination to a future glory.

- He **predestined us to adoption as sons** through Jesus Christ to Himself, according to the kind intention of His will" [Eph. 1:5].

The "us" of Eph. 1:5 refers to those "in Him" or "in Christ" as the context of Ephesians proves. Verse 13 establishes that Paul's remarks concern all believers. **Believers**, then, are **predestined to adoption** or *son placing*. What is Paul's definition of adoption or son-placing? Rom. 8:23 gives the answer:

- And not only this, but also we ourselves having the first fruits of the Spirit, even we ourselves groan within ourselves waiting eagerly for our **adoption as sons, the redemption of our body** [Rom. 8:23].

Rom. 8:23 teaches that one aspect of this "**son-placing**" **is the total redemption of the body from the affects and presence of sin.**[1] There is a future

---

[1] "Son-placing" is a literal (admittedly awkward) translation of the Greek word but does have the advantage of showing that the word goes far beyond the initial entrance into the family unlike the English term *adoption*. Paul's full definition includes a time of mature sonship when **one already in the family becomes a full son** in the sense of outgrowing status as a minor child and gaining full rights as an adult son. The author knows of no an-

aspect of the adoption of sons where the children of God will become mature sons like Christ Jesus and will obtain their inheritance. The ideas of obtaining an inheritance and being redeemed from the curse of sin are all in the context of Romans 8. This future adoption of Rom. 8:23 equals being mature sons conformed to the image of His Son in Rom. 8:29. Therefore, Romans 8 teaches that **believers are predestined** to a full adoption as sons when they will obtain an inheritance, **become like Jesus Christ**, and be redeemed physically from the affects of sin. Being predestined to adoption as sons means believers are predestined to be like the Lord Jesus Christ in glory and sinless perfection. There could not be a stronger statement of eternal security.

In the context of Ephesians 1:5 a future aspect to "adoption of sons" must also be intended. Just as in Romans 8, Ephesians 1 deals with inheritance (vv. 11 and 14) and seems to refer to the redemption of the believer's body (v. 14). Ephesians 1 clearly has a future orientation, and there is no reason for missing a parallel with Romans 8. The author is the same and in both places the subject is "adoption as sons" and predestination. **Take careful note that in both Romans 8 and Ephesians 1 a believer is predestined**

---

cient ceremonies of placement as adult sons, but the concept is similar to a bar mitzvah when one already a son becomes acknowledged as a mature son. Believers are predestined not just to entrance into God's family but to become sinless and perfect (mature sons) like the Lord Jesus Christ.

**to obtain a full mature *sonship*.**

Those who deny the eternal security of the believer must disagree that a believer is predestined to glory. They must deny the believer is predestined to obtain a full "adoption as sons." Since God has made the decree that those justified are as good as glorified and has decreed those "in Christ" will obtain adoption as sons, (i.e. inheritance, redemption of the body, full sonship after the image of Christ), those who deny security unknowingly deny that God can or will abide by His own promises. If a believer does not obtain glory or full "sonship", then either God contradicted Himself, or He is not able to keep His self-imposed obligation. Either God was mistaken in these teachings about predestination to glory, or He does not have the power or ability to guarantee a full adoption as sons. If a Christian can lose salvation, then God is not all-powerful and the Bible is in error on the topic of predestination.

### *If a Christian loses salvation by misdeeds or a lack of works, then salvation would be based upon works*

Few truths are clearer than the idea that salvation is not granted on the basis of works. The denial that salvation is secure ultimately leads back to a works-salvation. Many who espouse the "insecurity" of the believer claim this is an untrue distortion and misrepresentation of their viewpoint. They would deny salvation by works. They would insist that salvation is initially granted as a free gift through faith, but that

# YOU ARE INVITED TO THE FIRST ANNUAL

ARCOS RESTAURANT
129
S. Broadway

# HOLIDAY PARTY
## DEC 21 8:00pm
### LIVE MUSIC
### ALL NIGHT HAPPY HOUR
### FREE BUFFET
**410-522-4777**
**EMAIL— Arcos129@Gmail.com**

# ARCOS NEW YEARS EVE PARTY
## DRINK SPECIALS ALL NIGHT!!
## TEQUILA ICE LUGE!!

**HAPPY HOUR EVERYDAY 5-7 PM**
**$3.50 MARGARITA**
**$2.50 CORONA**
FRI & SAT NIGHT—TACOS PASTOR

**FOR MORE INFO**
**CALL 410-522-4777 OR**
**ARCOS129@GMAIL.COM**

## December 2005

| SUN | MON | TUE | WED | THU | FRI | SAT |
|---|---|---|---|---|---|---|
| 11<br>FAMILY NIGHT<br>KIDS EAT FREE | 12<br>CLOSED | 13<br>HOPKINS EMPLOYEE NIGHT<br>10% OFF | 14<br>LUNCH SPECIALS | 15<br>2 FOR 1 TEQUILA SHOTS | 16<br>LIVE X-MAS MARIA-CHI | 17<br>SINGLES NIGHT |
| 18<br>FAMILY NIGHT<br>KIDS EAT FREE | 19<br>CLOSED | 20<br>HOPKINS EMPLOYEE NIGHT<br>10% OFF | **ARCOS X-MAS FIESTA** | 22<br>2 FOR 1 MEXICAN BEER | 23<br>LUNCH SPECIALS | 24<br>SINGLES NIGHT |
| 25<br>CLOSED | 26<br>CLOSED | 27<br>HOPKINS NIGHT<br>10% OFF | 28<br>LUNCH SPECIALS | 29<br>2 FOR 1 EVERY-THING!! | 30<br>LIVE MARIA-CHI BAND | **NEW YEARS EVE!!** |

SUN— ONE CHILD (UNDER 12) PER ADULT
TUES — WITH VALID PROOF
THUR— AFTER 7 PM / NO TOP SHELF

# ARCOS NEW YEARS EVE PARTY
## DRINK SPECIALS ALL NIGHT!!
## TEQUILA ICE LUGE!!

**HAPPY HOUR EVERYDAY 5-7 PM**
**$3.50 MARGARITA**
**$2.50 CORONA**
FRI & SAT NIGHT—TACOS PASTOR

**FOR MORE INFO**
**CALL 410-522-4777 OR**
**ARCOS129@GMAIL.COM**

## December 2005

| SUN | MON | TUE | WED | THU | FRI | SAT |
|---|---|---|---|---|---|---|
| 11 FAMILY NIGHT KIDS EAT FREE | 12 CLOSED | 13 HOPKINS EMPLOYEE NIGHT 10% OFF | 14 LUNCH SPECIALS | 15 2 FOR 1 TEQUILA SHOTS | 16 LIVE X-MAS MARIA-CHI | 17 SINGLES NIGHT |
| 18 FAMILY NIGHT KIDS EAT FREE | 19 CLOSED | 20 HOPKINS EMPLOYEE NIGHT 10% OFF | ARCOS X-MAS FIESTA | 22 2 FOR 1 MEXICAN BEER | 23 LUNCH SPECIALS | 24 SINGLES NIGHT |
| 25 CLOSED | 26 CLOSED | 27 HOPKINS NIGHT 10% OFF | 28 LUNCH SPECIALS | 29 2 FOR 1 EVERY-THING!! | 30 LIVE MARIA-CHI BAND | NEW YEARS EVE!! |

SUN— ONE CHILD (UNDER 12) PER ADULT
TUES — WITH VALID PROOF
THUR— AFTER 7 PM / NO TOP SHELF

# YOU ARE INVITED TO
# THE FIRST ANNUAL

ARCOS
RESTAURANT
129
S. Broadway

# HOLIDAY PARTY
# DEC 21 8:00pm
## LIVE MUSIC
### ALL NIGHT HAPPY HOUR
### FREE BUFFET
## 410-522-4777
### EMAIL — Arcos129@Gmail.com

subsequent to salvation a person must maintain a certain level of righteousness to maintain salvation. However, this is still a *works* system.

If God bestows initial salvation without effort but then requires us to perform in order to maintain salvation, then salvation is not a gift at all but is something we must work to have. There is not much difference between such a system and a car dealer who gives a car without cost but expects the recipient to work faithfully or make payments in order to maintain possession of that car. Such a relationship is not that of a free gift. It is a **contract of works**. If a Christian must work at righteousness to maintain possession of salvation, then the possession of salvation ultimately rests on works even if one claims it is initially given freely. **Salvation is a gift**. It is freely given by grace through faith in the Lord Jesus Christ. Works play no role in either obtaining or maintaining the possession of salvation.

- But to the one who does not work, but believes in Him who justifies the ungodly, his faith is reckoned as righteousness [Rom. 4:5].

- For by grace you have been saved through faith; and that not of yourselves, it is the gift of God; not as a result of works, that no one should boast [Eph. 2:8-9].

- He saved us, not on the basis of deeds which we have done in righteousness, but according to His mercy; by the washing of regeneration and renewing by the Holy Spirit [Titus 3:5].

## *If a Christian loses salvation and goes to hell because of sin, then Christ's atonement must not have perfectly dealt with all sins*

Again many who deny eternal security would be unaware that their position implies some defect in the cross. However, if a soul can lose his salvation due to sin and spend eternity in hell, then it must also be the case that there are some sins for which the price was not paid. These are the sins for which the ex-child of God would be suffering in hell. If a Christian can lose salvation and suffer punishment because of sins, then somehow Christ's work on the cross must not have completely solved the sin problem as it pertains to those "life-losing" sins. He must have died for some of that believer's sins but not all of them. There must be some sins that a believer might potentially commit that he could be liable for and would be required to suffer for them.

The idea that the cross did not completely solve the sin problem and that potentially a believer himself might have to pay for some sins is an insult to Christ's work on the cross. It means that there are some potential sins for which redemption has not been paid, but the Scripture speaks of redemption for the believer as involving a complete release from the slave market of sin that has already occurred. (See

Gal. 3:13, past tense; Titus 2:14, redeemed from **all** wickedness; Heb. 9:12, eternal redemption; Eph. 1:7, redemption already a possession; 1 Pet. 1:18,19, redemption past tense). The possibility of sins existing for which a Christian must spend eternity under God's wrath means that the cross did not fully propitiate God's wrath over sin, but the Scriptures teach otherwise (see Rom. 3:25; 1 John 2:1-2, 4:10). Either there has been redemption or there has not been redemption. Either there has been a propitiation of God's wrath or there has not been a propitiation of God's wrath. Either Christ's death finished the sin problem, or it did not (see John 19:30). Either Christ's sacrifice was complete and final or partial and tentative. Either it was completely sufficient or only partially sufficient. (See Heb. 9:12, 26, 28a, 10:10, 12,14.) The view that Christ's atonement completely dealt with the sin problem of the human race entails a belief that there are no more sins for which a believer might have to suffer. The view that there are potential sins for which a believer might be liable for eternal punishment entails the idea that the cross's remedy for sin was partial not total.

- [w]ho gave Himself for us, that He might redeem us from **every** lawless deed and purify for Himself a people for His own possession, zealous for good deeds [Titus 2:14].

- And when you were dead in your transgressions and the uncircumcision of your flesh, He made you alive together with Him, having forgiven us **all** our transgressions [Col. 2:13].

## *If a Christian can lose salvation, then God the Son can fail as an intercessor or advocate*

In John 17:11 Christ prays, "Holy Father keep them in Thy Name..." In the context Christ is referring to a keeping, guarding, preserving from perdition (see v. 12), and He is including within the scope of His prayer not just the apostles but all believers (see v. 20). Therefore, Christ has prayed that believers in Him be preserved from destruction. If a believer can ultimately perish, then Christ in John 17 made a request that was out of God's will and Christ failed as an intercessor. He made a petition to God the Father and was turned away.

The Lord Jesus Christ still intercedes on behalf of believers (Rom. 8:34; Heb. 7:24-25). He apparently is still asking for a safeguarding of believers. Heb. 7:25 teaches that a Savior who always lives is able to intercede at all times. This constant intercession results in an eternal salvation. God the Father honors Christ's never-ending petition on behalf of believers. John 11:42 teaches that the Father always hears the Son. Christ's life that never ends results in an intercession that never ends which in turn results in a salvation that never ends. Can we imagine Christ interceding for 2,000 years with a request that is periodically denied because it is not in God will? Of course not. It is within God's will that believers be kept, and He always honors the Son's request to do so.

- [b]ut He, on the other hand, because He abides forever, holds His priesthood permanently. Hence, also, He is able to **save forever** those who drew near to God through Him, since He always lives to make intercession for them [Heb. 7:24-25].

Christ's work as our Intercessor is related to His work as our Advocate. Satan is the accuser of the brethren (Rev. 12:10), but at each accusation of sin Christ our Lord is our defense attorney contending on our behalf (1 John 2:1). His defense does not fail.

*If a Christian loses salvation, then the Holy Spirit fails in His sealing ministry.*

- [w]ho also **sealed** us and gave us the Spirit in our hearts as a **pledge** [ 2 Cor. 1:22].

- In Him, you also, after listening to the message of truth, the gospel of your salvation - having also believed, you were **sealed** in Him with the Holy Spirit of promise, who is given as a **pledge** of our inheritance, with a view to the redemption of God's own possession, to the praise of His glory [Eph. 1:13-14].

- And do not grieve the Holy Spirit of God, by whom you were **sealed for the day of**

**redemption** [Eph. 4:30].

Several times Paul teaches that the Holy Spirit **seals** a believer (2 Cor. 1:22; Eph. 1:13-14, 4:30). In ancient times a seal with its impressed mark signified ownership and authority. The king's seal on a document meant authority. A seal on an object, such as an oil jar or wine flask, signified ownership. There is also the idea of approval or endorsement (John 3:33). Even today one can hear of a "seal of approval." Finally, sealing spoke of protection. The Lord's tomb was sealed to be protected (Matt. 27:66). A document would be sealed to be protected. The breaking of a seal might subject a document such as a will or title deed to alteration. Therefore, only a person with authority could break a legal seal (Rev. 5:9).

The sealing of the Spirit refers to God's ownership, approval, and protection of a believer. Are there limits to this protection? Eph. 4:30 teaches that believers are **sealed for the day of redemption**, i.e., until the redemption of our bodies when we obtain glory and full inheritance. The Holy Spirit throughout this earthly life seals believers. The duration of the Spirit's protection or time-span of His ownership extends all the way to glorification. If a Christian can lose salvation, then the seal of the Holy Spirit could be broken off long before the day of redemption. If a Christian can lose salvation, then Eph. 4:30 would be an error.

Both 2 Cor. 1:22 and Eph. 1:13-14 mention the

Holy Spirit as a pledge in the same sentence that refers to His sealing work (see also 2 Cor. 5:5). The
Holy Spirit is said to be the earnest or pledge of our
full inheritance. The King James word *earnest* is
somewhat archaic. The phrase "down-payment"
communicates better. The underlying Greek word
means "engagement ring" in modern Greek. The
Holy Spirit is like a down payment or engagement
ring. He is the pledge, promise or guarantee of
greater blessings to come. Another term that ex-
presses the same truth is *first-fruits* (Rom. 8:23). The
Holy Spirit is the guarantee and beginning of greater
blessing in the future. His role of sealing until the
day of redemption means that the Holy Spirit is a
secure and certain pledge that future blessing will be
obtained. Yet, if a Christian loses salvation, then the
Holy Spirit was not the first-fruits of a future blessing, and He was not the down-payment or pledge of a
greater inheritance. If the Holy Spirit does indeed
seal for the day of redemption and if He is the pledge
of a greater inheritance, then eternal security follows.

## *If a Christian can lose salvation, it makes the prom-ises of the Bible untrue*

The Bible teaches that a believer will not suffer
condemnation and is not subject to God's eternal
wrath. Yet, if a Christian loses salvation, then he is
subject to condemnation and God's eternal wrath.

- "Truly, truly, I say to you, he who hears
  My word, and believes Him who sent Me,

has eternal life, and does not come into judgment, but has passed out of death into life" [John 5:24].

- There is, therefore, now no condemnation for those who are in Christ Jesus [Rom. 8:1].

- Much more then, having now been justified by His blood, we shall be saved from the wrath of God through Him [Rom 5:9].

- For God has not destined us for wrath but for obtaining salvation through our Lord Jesus Christ [1 Thess. 5:9].

If a believer's ultimate salvation is a variable, then John 5:24 ought to read, "He who hears My word and believes Him who sent Me *might* have eternal life and *probably* will not come into condemnation but *likely* has passed out of death into life." Rom. 8:1 ought to say, "There will *probably* not be condemnation to those who are in Christ."

Heb. 13:5 says, "I will never leave you nor forsake you." If a believer could lose salvation, then Christ would leave him. Heb. 13:5 promises He will never leave. (The Greek phrase has *five* negatives)

John 6:37 says "the one who comes to Me I will certainly not cast out" (double negative in the Greek for emphasis). Those who teach a believer can lose salvation should consider what is really being promised here. Indeed, the phrase **has eternal life** is common (e.g., John 6:47). If a person has a life that can end, that life, by definition, was never eternal in the first place. Christ teaches that the one who believes already possesses eternal life. By definition this means his life will not end.

Rom. 8:38-39 says **nothing** can separate the believer from the love of Christ. If a Christian can lose salvation, then **something** must cause separation. Likewise, in John 10:28 Christ promises, "They shall never perish" (double negative again). If a believer loses salvation and perishes, then this promise is also wrong. A believer who loses salvation would never have possessed eternal life. He would come into judgment and be subject to God's eternal wrath. God would forsake the ex-child of God, he would be cast out, he would be separated from God's love, and he would perish. The Bible will not allow these possibilities.

*If a Christian can lose salvation then God has failed in His intention to keep us.*

- [t]o obtain an inheritance which is imperishable and undefiled and will not fade away, **reserved** in heaven for you who are **protected** by the power of God through faith for a salvation ready to be revealed in the last time [1 Pet. 1:4-5].

- Now to Him who is able to **keep** you from stumbling, and to make you stand in the presence of His glory blameless with great joy [Jude v. 24].

If a Christian can lose salvation, then heaven is *not* reserved *nor* are all believers protected by God's power. If a Christian can lose salvation, then God does *not* keep him from stumbling or bring him into glory. Yet, these two passages present a sovereign God whose intention is to protect and preserve believers in the faith and from falling.

*If a Christian can lose salvation, the Bible is confusing for it does not specify any causes that remove salvation*

There is **no** teaching in the Bible that lists the kind of sin that removes salvation or what degree of sin exposes a risk to loss of salvation. Unless eternal security is true, it would be inconceivable that God would delete all instruction about forfeiture of salvation. He would want His people to be warned of specific perils. Yet, there are no such warnings. Instead 1 Cor. 3:15 indicates that all believers, even those who are lacking in good works will be saved at the Judgment Seat of Christ:

- If any man's work is burned up, he shall suffer loss, but he himself shall be saved… [1Cor. 3:15].

## If we view the subject from a positive standpoint - Eternal Security is true

To this point we have viewed the subject of eternal security negatively, looking at the absurdities and inconsistencies that would be true if salvation could be lost. Perhaps it is best to review the same truths phrased from a positive standpoint. Eternal security, then, is true for the following nine reasons:

### *Christ's righteousness saves (not our own righteousness); one cannot lose salvation*

Justification by faith means that Christ's righteousness saves a believer. Since He will never lose His righteousness, a believer can never lose his justification.

### *Election and predestination prove eternal security*

The Bible's teaching on election and predestination prove eternal security. Those whom God has justified are as good as already glorified.

### *Salvation is not given or maintained by good works.*

Salvation is not initially given because of good works, nor do good works maintain it.

### *Christ's atonement is perfect and complete*

Christ's atonement is perfect and complete. He has paid for all sin. There is no sin that remains for which a believer could ever suffer.

### *Christ as advocate guarantees security*

Christ's ministries as intercessor and advocate guarantee security.

### *The Holy Spirit's seal cannot be broken*

The Holy Spirit has sealed believers until the day of redemption. This seal cannot be broken. He is also our pledge and guarantee of a future inheritance.

## *Many promises guarantee security*

There are many promises that guarantee eternal life without condemnation. Eternal life by the definition of *eternal* cannot end.

## *God is able to keep us from falling*

God says He is able to keep us from falling and that we are kept by His power.

## *There are no Scriptural grounds for losing salvation*

The Bible never gives any grounds for losing salvation. Even believers with unproductive lives and few good works obtain salvation at the Judgment Seat of Christ.

# **Problem Passages Explained**

In theological circles those who deny eternal security are called Arminians after the Dutch theologian Jacob (James) Arminius (1560-1609). Most groups coming from the Wesleyan tradition such as Methodists are Arminian in that they disagree with eternal security. This issue is not among the fundamentals of the faith, but the security of the believer is among the most important doctrines that divide believers. Thinking Arminians use Bible texts to prove a Christian can lose salvation. However, each of these texts can also be interpreted in ways compatible with eternal security.

**Psalm 51:11** (See also Judges 16:20 and 1 Sam. 16:14)

- Do not cast me away from Thy presence, and do not take Thy Holy Spirit from me [Psa. 51:11].

David seems worried that the Holy Spirit would leave him. Under the Law system the Holy Spirit did not indwell every believer (John 7:39) nor had God promised the Holy Spirit would indwell forever (e.g., John 14:16-17). Unlike the Spirit's ministry since Pentecost (Acts 2), the Holy Spirit might depart from a believer under the Law of Moses. This would result in ineffective living and ministry but not a loss of salvation. Another interpretation would take "spirit" as a reference to David's own spirit. He would be saying, "please do not take the spirit of holiness away from my life." In other words, do not let me lose strong conviction over sin or the desire for holiness in my life. Don't give up on me. Keep convicting me and making me want holiness.

Chapter 10 of the complete doctrinal study, *Not By Bread Alone; An Outlined Guide to Bible Doctrine*, includes detailed studies on the changes in the Holy Spirit's ministry since Pentecost (in Acts 2). [2]

---

[2] An alternative view would hold that the Holy Spirit did indwell all Old Testament believers. He would also come upon leaders

**Ezekiel 33:12-20** (See also Ezek. 3:20; 18:20)

• "And you, son of man, say to your fellow
  citizens, 'The righteousness of a righteous
  man will not deliver him in the day of his
  transgression, and as for the wickedness of
  the wicked, he will not stumble because of
  it in the day when he turns from his wickedness; whereas a righteous man will not
  be able to live by his righteousness on the
  day when he commits sin' " ... "When I say
  to the righteous he will surely live, and he
  so trusts in his righteousness that he commits iniquity, none of his righteous deeds
  will be remembered; but in that same iniquity of his which he has committed he will
  surely die" [Ezek. 33:12-13].

Ezekiel's warnings about death from sin involve
physical death (either capital punishment as in 18:20,
or death in war with Israel's enemies). Ezekiel 33
concerns a predicted attack with a "sword upon the
land" (v. 2). God promised deliverance for those living in righteousness at the time of destruction. He
warns of death for those living in wickedness. The
question of eternal salvation is not the issue here.
Death refers to physical death because of sin. Several
other references that can be misunderstood may also
concern physical death.

---

for special empowerment. One could conclude David fears a loss
of this special anointing of the Holy Spirit for leaders.

**Matthew 24:13** (See also Matt. 10:22; Mark 13:13; Luke 21:19)

- "But the one who endures to the end, he shall be saved" [Matt. 24:13].

- "By your endurance you will gain your lives" [Luke 21:19].

Salvation in these verses could be physical deliverance or spiritual deliverance. With either interpretation the key to understanding is putting the statement in its tribulational setting. The Lord refers to the period of suffering just before the Second Coming. Matt. 24:21 says, "...for then there shall be a **great tribulation**, such as has not occurred since the beginning of the world until now, nor ever shall." This absolutely unique period will be a time of great persecution of believers with much loss of physical life. Also, everyone will be forced to demonstrate allegiance to the evil end-time dictator by accepting a bodily mark. Refusal of the mark is a certain indication of faith in Christ and will result in unavoidable suffering, (Rev. 13:16-18). Thus, it can be said that those who endure persecution from the Antichrist gain spiritual salvation. This salvation does not come on the basis of the good work of endurance. Rather the decision to trust in Christ, even though it results in persecution brings salvation. Endurance of persecution in the Tribulation will not earn or retain salvation, but it does demonstrate it. To believe will mean to endure suffering. To endure will mean to believe.

All others will submit to worshiping a false christ. It is difficult to know whether the Lord intends physical salvation or spiritual salvation.

## *Physical salvation (rescue) from the Tribulation*

The Lord's words might be taken as encouragement that the Tribulation period has limited duration. It will not last indefinitely. Those who are able to endure persecution will find a rescue (physical salvation) at the end of the period by the Lord's return to the earth. [3] These may be words of hope and encouragement to tribulational saints. There will be an end to the ordeal. The Lord will return in power to destroy their tormentors and to rescue (save) believers from further suffering.

## *Spiritual salvation*

The NASB translation of Luke 21:19 seems to favor physical deliverance. In the Luke context, v. 19 could even be a promise that those apostles still living in A.D. 70 would survive the destruction of Jerusalem even though some other believers would die (v. 16). However, the Greek phraseology in Luke seems harder to limit to physical rescue (salvation) at the end of the Tribulation period than is the parallel in Matt. 24:13.

- "By your endurance you will gain your souls" [Luke 21:19 (literal translation)].

---

[3] The *end* in this view refers to the end of the Tribulation period. In the next view *end* refers to the end of life.

In Luke 21:16 the Lord says, "They will put some of you to death." Then in v. 18 He says, "Yet, not a hair on your head shall perish." This sounds as if Christ intends to contrast physical death with spiritual salvation. "They may kill you, but they cannot really harm you spiritually." Assuming Luke 21:19 refers to a spiritual salvation, it still could not possibly be referring to a loss of salvation. If it does, it would also be teaching good works earns salvation. Clearly, there has to be a better way to understand these two passages. As a background, we must first consider the nature of saving faith and the conditions in the Tribulation period.

<u>Saving faith</u>

Genuine believers are kept in faith. Believers *believe*. A more complete discussion of this conclusion will occur under a following problem passage (1 Cor. 15:1-2; Col. 1:21-23). Jesus says in John 10:5 that his sheep "do not know the voice of strangers." A Christian might deny faith to others in situations of embarrassment or danger as did Peter. However, Peter never denied Christ to God the Father or denied Christ in his own heart. Genuine believers do not deny Christ is the Son of God or that He died for our sins and rose again. In the conditions of the Tribulation, this means that genuine believers will not worship the Antichrist or accept his mark.

<u>Tribulational conditions</u>

When the Tribulation begins everyone on earth

will be unsaved. [4] After the Antichrist assumes dictatorial powers over the world, he will force all people to choose between worshiping himself or worshiping the true Christ (Matt. 24:15; 2 Thess. 2:4; Rev. 13:15-18). Also, God will indirectly participate in the process. Those who will not receive the truth of Christ will be blinded so as to believe the Antichrist's lies (2 Thess. 2:11-12). Pressures, both Satanic and divine, will force all people to choose. During the Tribulation, some who began the period as unsaved will turn to faith in Christ (the saints mentioned in Daniel and Revelation, e.g., Rev. 7:9,14). Virtually no other time in world history has required faith to be demonstrated in such a permanent irrevocable way. The decision to accept the beast's mark is a final unchangeable rejection of Christ. All unbelievers will eventually give in to the Antichrist's power and worship him, sealing their choice with a bodily mark. By contrast, only believers and all believers will refuse. A true believer will not be able to reject Christ in such a permanent and final sense. Instead, believers will demonstrate faith by rejecting the mark and incurring the hatred of the Antichrist. **Of the Tribulation period it will be true to say that those who are still enduring the beast's persecution at the end are the genuinely saved ones.** They do not earn or keep salvation by perseverance.

---

[4] This assumes the pretribulational Rapture for which arguments are given in Chapter 12 of *Not By Bread Alone; An Outlined Guide to Bible Doctrine.*

They reveal or display their faith. Saving faith leads to refusal to worship the beast or accept his permanent mark of allegiance. The individuals who refuse to worship the beast through to the end of the Tribulation are the identical individuals who gain salvation by trusting Christ instead. Because of the choice to trust Christ and thereby reject Antichrist, they have inevitable suffering, but they also have gained salvation. Those who choose faith in Christ will endure suffering and likely death but will also gain their souls by their choice. Those who choose to worship the beast and accept his mark do not lose salvation; they demonstrate they **never had salvation**. We could paraphrase Jesus' words this way. "Those who persevere to the end against the Antichrist are the saved ones." The truth can also be stated, "he that is saved will endure". This gives the same truth but with different emphasis. It would emphasize that every true believer will reject worshiping the Antichrist and suffer for that choice. Instead Jesus wanted to stress the positive. These will gain salvation by their choice to accept Christ (not Antichrist) even though it will entail persecution and often death.

## Matthew 25:30 (See also Matt. 8:11-12)

- "And cast out the worthless slave into the outer darkness; in that place there shall be weeping and gnashing of teeth" [Matt. 25:30].

  Here we have a case of a servant ending up in

outer darkness. Is this a warning of a Christian losing salvation? The church does not begin until Acts 2. Though many of the Lord's teachings look forward to the church dispensation, many other statements are directed at Israel. In a sense all Jews were servants of God, but not all Jews were saved. Many had no faith. Thus, a Jewish servant of God could end up in punishment. However, this would not be an example of a believer in Christ losing salvation. The context of Matt. 8:12 proves the Lord has unbelieving Israel in mind.

### John 15:1-8

- I am the true vine, and My Father is the vinedresser. Every branch in Me that does not bear fruit, He takes away; and every branch that bears fruit, He prunes it, that it may bear more fruit. You are already clean because of the word, which I have spoken to you. Abide in Me, and I in you. As the branch cannot bear fruit of itself, unless it abides in the vine, so neither can you, unless you abide in Me. I am the vine, you the branches; he who abides in Me, and I in him, he bears much fruit; for apart from Me you can do nothing. If anyone does not abide in Me, he is thrown away as a branch, and dries up; and they gather them, and cast them into the fire, and they are burned. If you abide in Me, and My words abide in you, ask whatever you wish, and it shall be done for you. By this is My Father glorified, that you bear much fruit, and so prove to be My disciples [John 15:1-8].

The cut and discarded branch of John 15 has been taken to be a believer who loses salvation. However, there are other views, which handle the passage in ways that preserve eternal security. It could be an explanation of the departure of Judas from the apostolic company, or it could be a warning about the believer's chastisement in this life.

## *Judas as the cut branch*

Perhaps John 15 is closely directed to the original listeners. The broken and discarded branch explains Judas' departure earlier that same evening (see John 13:26-30). The call to abide directs the other apostles to remain in the faith and to keep true to Christ during the coming arrest, trial, and death. While lessons can be drawn for all times, many contextual clues show the Lord's teaching is mainly addressed to those from the upper room who had just left the room and were moving toward the garden (cf. John 14:31 with 18:1). Meanwhile, Judas was betraying Jesus and would soon die. Consider the many hints that the Lord is speaking primarily of the apostles:

- "...He [the Holy Spirit] will teach you all things and bring to your remembrance all that I said to you" [John 14:26].

- "[a]nd you will bear witness also because you have been with me from the beginning" [John 15:27].

- "They will make you outcasts from the synagogue...." [John 16:2].

- "...And these things I did not say to you at the beginning because I was with you" [John 16:4b].

- "I have many more things to say to you but you cannot bear them now" [John 16:12].

- "I do not ask in behalf of these alone but for those also who will believe in Me through their Word" [John 17:20].

The Upper Room Discourse seems directed primarily at the disciples. No Christian today was with the Lord "from the beginning" (John 15:27 or 16:4). Even John 17:20, which mentions those in following generations who would believe in Christ because of the apostolic message, reinforces the idea that the Lord's teachings are directed mainly at the apostles. If we view John 15 as primarily directed at the apostles, then the Lord is explaining Judas' departure and commanding the remaining apostles to keep the faith in the dark days immediately ahead.

John 15:2 speaks of a fruitless branch that is taken

away. [5] Though it is visibly connected to the vine (as outwardly Judas had been connected to Christ by association), there was no interchange of life from within. Life did not flow from the vine to this dead branch. Therefore, God took it away (removed) it. Though outwardly tied to Christ, Judas had never absorbed life from Christ. He is not an example of a believer who loses salvation. He is an example of one who is outwardly associated with Christianity but has no inward life. Verse two tells the disciples that the fruitless and dead Judas had just been removed from all association with Christ. He would also soon be taken away in death.

The remaining disciples are like the branch that produces some fruit. In addition to mere outward association, they have an inner connection (union) with the Lord Jesus. Life flows from Him to them. They can expect pruning (hardships and/or chastisement) which will produce more fruit.

In John 15:4 Jesus commands the remaining apostles to "abide in Me." The command to "abide" includes an appeal to a deeper relationship of keeping all the Lord's commandments. It is a command to

---

[5] The phrase "in Me" seems to refer to outward association. There were two kinds of branches in Christ. First, dead branches who had no inner connection and no life. Second, branches with fruit who possessed a living connection on the inside. Only those in the second category could keep the command to abide. Dead branches have visible connection to Christianity but no life. They cannot abide in a relationship they do not possess.

absorb more intimate life from the vine. This is the definition of abide in 1 John 3:24. The command to abide includes more than the topic of salvation and encompasses obedience (see 15:5,10). However, the command to abide does not include less than the topic of salvation either. [6] Abide means remain. While Jesus is telling His apostles to keep His commandments, He is also calling them to remain in the faith during the difficult times just ahead.

Why would one who accepts eternal security think Jesus would need to tell the apostles to remain in faith? One of God's methods for keeping believers in the faith (1 Pet. 1:4-5) is by Scriptural commands to remain in the faith. In a hypothetical sense one might lose faith and salvation with it were it not for God's work of preserving a believer in the faith. If it were not for Jesus' gracious warning and commands

---

[6] In 1 John 4:15 "abide in Him" seems to be the equivalent to being saved, perhaps also 1 John 2:6 (where "abide" equals "in Him" in v. 5). In 1 John 3:24 to abide means to keep the Lord's commandments. Both ideas may be included in John 15. Jesus is not telling unbelievers to enter salvation (though the text could be applied this way in modern sermons). He is commanding the saved apostles to remain in the relationship they already possess, i.e., keep the faith they have, and also to obey His commandments. It is not the case that Judas stopped abiding. Only the living branches could abide. They would abide by staying in faith and by obedience. There are two types of branches "in Me" (i.e. associated with Christ outwardly). Those connected visibly but lacking fruit are dead. Those connected visibly bearing some fruit are alive. Only the living branches have a union in which they could remain and grow deeper.

in John 15, perhaps the apostles would have abandoned their faith during this critical period. However, the Lord intended to keep them secure by not letting this happen. The very command for the disciples to remain (abide) in the faith exhibits God's means of keeping these men in the faith during the dark night and fateful crucifixion day soon to come. Is not this what the Lord means in John 16:1? By application to modern times, we see that Scriptural commands to keep faith are not incompatible with the doctrine of eternal security. Commands to remain in faith in Christ are one means God uses to keep believers secure. When the Lord commanded the apostles to abide, He included both the ideas of remaining in the faith and keeping His commandments.

This command is not really directed to Judas or people like him. Like a dead branch associated by connection to a vine, Judas had been outwardly connected to Jesus without any inner life. Judas will not abide because Judas cannot abide. One cannot keep what one does not have in the first place. Judas could not abide in Christ because He could not remain in a faith that had never begun. He could neither preserve a living union with Christ nor enter a more intimate union by keeping all Christ's commandments. Judas is the dead branch thrown into the fire.

He may illustrate a type of person today who is outwardly tied to Christ by association, such as church membership, but still lacks faith. Without faith there is no spiritual union. Such a person cannot

abide because he cannot continue (abide) in a relationship he has not yet begun. He certainly cannot
deepen that relationship by keeping the Lord's commandments unless he trusts in Christ. He will eventually, like Judas, be severed from all tenuous links
that only appear to be tied to Christ and be thrown
into flames.

By interpreting John 15 closely in its original setting, we have found the text need not involve a genuine Christian who loses salvation. Judas is the dead
branch. He did not lose salvation. He **never had** salvation. He did not abide and then lose salvation. He
could not abide because he could not remain (much
less deepen) in a relationship he never possessed.
Judas is a warning for all those outwardly associating
with the things of Christ but without real union by
faith.

Many who accept eternal security will not accept
the above interpretation of John 15. They would pre-
fer that fire not be a reference to eternal punishment.
Neither would they understand the command to abide
to include an appeal to remain in the faith. For them
fire speaks of loss of rewards and/or temporal chastisement of the believer. The call to abide is a call to
deeper and full obedience that has nothing to do with
remaining in the faith. While the author prefers the
"Judas View," this second view is worthy of respect.

### *Warning of chastisement, loss of rewards view*

Perhaps John 15 is not referring to a "Judas-type"

who has associations with Christianity, but no faith. If Christ's words exclusively concern believers, then He is warning believers to abide in a life of obedience and full allegiance. Those who refuse may endure chastisement, even unto physical death, and loss of rewards.

John 15:2 speaks of those "in Me" who bear no fruit and those who bear some fruit. [7] Christians who are void of productivity may be taken away from this world in physical death (cf. 1 Cor. 11:30). Christians who yield some productivity for Christ can expect hardship (pruning) to increase productivity.

The call to abide in v. 4 is a command to keep Christ's commandments.

> "And the one who keeps His commandments abides in Him...."[1 John 3:24] (see also 1 John 2:28).

Those who refuse to keep His commandments are like the branch of v. 6. Burning could be an agricultural metaphor. Farmers burn a field to purify it from

---

[7] Unlike the "Judas View," the chastisement view would interpret both types of branches in v. 2 as saved. Both would have inner spiritual union. There would be saved branches "in Me" with no fruit and other saved branches that produce fruit. However, just as with the "Judas View", the phrase "in Me" in v. 2 would not be identical with abiding. It would still be the case that those "in Me" might not be abiding, i.e. keeping the commandments.

weeds and increase productivity.[8] Those who will not abide will face God's purifying chastisement. This is not the loss of salvation but rather troubles designed to improve the believer. Also, there could be a reference here to loss of rewards.

1 Cor. 3:15 says at the Judgment Seat a believer might find some of his life's work burned up. He himself is still saved but loses rewards. This second possible interpretation of the nature of burning in John 15:6 avoids any contradiction with texts which teach eternal security. It also has the advantage of being simple and includes John's definition of abiding as obedience in 1 John 3:24.[9] The author believes the previous view pays closer attention to the original setting and has a better explanation of the branch in the fire metaphor. Regardless of the interpretation one prefers, it ought to be evident that John 15:1-8 need not contradict eternal security.

---

[8] The author believes that the burning in Heb. 6:8 does speak of the burning of a believer in chastisement. However, notice that in Hebrews 6 the illustration is of a field. Fire burns off weeds and impurities from a field and improves a field's productivity without destroying it. However, John 15 uses a branch as an illustration. Fire would totally destroy a branch. The "Judas View" has an advantage in taking the warning to be that of Hell. Also, if fire equals chastisement in John 15:6 what does the pruning of verse two mean? Would it not be better to see chastisement as included in pruning (v. 2) with fire (v. 6) as a reference to an even more severe danger?

[9] However, 1 John 2:5-6 seems to take *abide* as reference to being saved.

## Romans 11:11-32

- You will say then, Branches were broken
  off so that I might be grafted in. Quite
  right, they were broken off for their unbelief, but you stand by your faith. Do not be
  conceited, but fear; for if God did not spare
  the natural branches, neither will He spare
  you. Behold then the kindness and severity
  of God; to those who fell, severity, but to
  you, God's kindness, if you continue in His
  kindness; otherwise you also will be cut
  off. And they also, if they do not continue
  in their unbelief, will be grafted in; for God
  is able to graft them in again [Rom. 11:19-
  23].

### *The Jew-Gentile issue*

Paul's question in Romans 11:1 concerns whether
God has rejected Israel. No, He has not rejected Israel because there is a believing remnant. However,
because of Jewish unbelief (v. 20) God has sus-
pended His work for Israel as a special people above
all others. Now God includes Gentiles in His place of
blessing. Israel as a nation was cut off from God's
place of blessing, but this does not allow Gentile ar-
rogance toward Israel. Paul explains that jealousy
over gentile blessing may lead some Jews to faith in
Christ (vv. 11, 14). In the future millennial Kingdom
God will return Israel to a special position (vv. 25-
27). In the meantime, Gentiles must not feel God's

attention upon them comes from superiority over Jews. In explaining the relationship between Jew and Gentile, Paul uses the illustration of an olive tree.

## *The original olive tree*

The olive tree in Romans 11 is not the church. In a general sense it is the place of God's favor, the place of spiritual opportunity and blessings. More specifically, the olive tree is the place of blessings through Abraham. Since the root is holy (Abraham and the Patriarchs) so are the branches (following generations of Jews especially those with faith). Gentiles owe all their spiritual benefits to Israel.

Note carefully that the original olive tree (Old Testament Judaism) held branches consisting of **saved and unsaved** Jews. Some of the Jewish branches were believers, but some had no faith (v. 20). Therefore, this tree is **not** the tree of salvation, but rather a tree that pictures a broad range of spiritual opportunities and blessings. Blessings stemming from Abraham include eternal salvation (only for those with faith). However, blessings from Abraham upon Jews include other areas such as abundant knowledge about God through the Scriptures and prophetic leaders, practical wisdom in terms of family, business and governmental relationships, and the blessings of ready access to God and living in a nation with many believers. Even the unsaved Israelites enjoyed many advantages.

However, because of unbelief God broke off all

unbelieving Jews from the place of special blessing. God abrogated the Law of Moses including Judaism. Removing these unbelieving Jews from a place of God's special attention did not involve a loss of salvation because those without faith never had salvation. The primary definition of "breaking off" a branch is not loss of salvation but rather hardening, (see vv. 7-25). The hardening of unbelieving Israel constitutes a breaking off from the place of special blessings for Israel.

## *The gentile relationship to the olive tree*

God removed unbelieving Israel as an object of special opportunity and privilege. God then extended opportunities and special blessings to all nations (gentiles). Just as the original tree had both saved and unsaved Jews, the merger of gentiles to the place of blessing involves saved and unsaved gentiles. In Romans 11, Paul addresses his readers as gentiles (see 11:13). The pronoun *you* in his argument addresses the Romans as gentiles. "They" refers to Jews. Just as with Judaism, even unsaved gentiles can benefit from Christianity through common blessings. Unsaved gentiles still can have access to truth through the Scriptures and through churches. Cultures which and individuals who adhere to Biblical ethics benefit in terms of the family, business, government, and criminal/judicial affairs. However, permanent blessings from God come only to those with faith. Verse 20 teaches that "you (gentiles) stand only by faith." The gentiles that do have per-

manent standing within the tree of God's blessing
possess their position by faith. No gentile must ever
think that God's interest in them has to do with in-
herent superiority over Jews. One can see the danger
of Romans looking down upon Jews. However, all
gentiles have a debt to Israel for truth in Jewish
Scriptures, Jewish prophets, and a Jewish Messiah
(v. 18).

The gentiles that do stand in a permanent place of
blessing do so only by faith (v. 20). However, unbelieving gentile Christians can no more be saved than
unbelieving Jews. There may be many temporary
blessings from Christian influence, and exposure to
Christian truth, but gentiles who lack faith will be cut
off from eternal blessings. The warning in verses 20-
22 does not involve a loss of salvation. Unbelieving
gentiles who share many blessings by God's work
among the gentiles face a danger of removal from all
blessing in this life and eternity. Cutting off would
not refer to a loss of salvation. Unbelievers are not
saved in the first place. The cutting off refers to a
hardening of unbelieving gentiles just as it refers to a
hardening of unbelieving Jews (vv. 7 and 25). Continuance of God's kindness comes only by faith (cf.,
Romans 2:4 where God's kindness leads to repentance). An unbeliever can experience God's temporary common grace, but only believers have continuance in eternal grace. The danger of being removed
from God's blessing comes from unbelief, (v. 20).
Being cut off from the place of blessing means re-

moval from temporary blessing such as Christian instruction and blindness to the truth. This is not a loss of salvation but does concern salvation. Unbelieving gentiles who are hardened, i.e., blind to truth can never believe and, therefore, have no hope of salvation.

### Conclusion

Romans 11:11-32 should not be used as an objection to eternal security. Branches cut off the olive tree are unbelievers being removed from exposure to God's blessing and being hardened in their unbelief. Common grace extends to all gentiles. However, only those with faith continue in God's grace for eternity (v. 20). Permanent blessings come by faith, not by any superiority of gentiles over Jews.

**1 Corinthians 6:9-10** (Gal. 5:19-21, See also Eph. 5:5)

- Or do you not know that the unrighteous shall not inherit the kingdom of God? Do not be deceived; neither fornicators, nor idolaters, nor adulterers, nor effeminate, nor homosexuals, nor thieves, nor the covetous, nor drunkards, nor revilers, nor swindlers, shall inherit the kingdom of God [1 Cor. 6:9-10].

- Now the deeds of the flesh are evident, which are: immorality, impurity, sensuality, idolatry, sorcery, enmities, strife, jealousy, outbursts of anger, disputes, dissensions, factions, envying, drunkenness, carousing, and things like these, of which I forewarn you just as I have forewarned you that those who **practice** such things shall not inherit the kingdom of God [Gal. 5:19-21].

(These texts are studied in more detail in *Not By Bread Alone; An Outlined Guide to Bible Doctrine*).

Paul's words mean that an ongoing "**practice**" of sin without conviction or repentance gives indication a person has never been saved. Christians are indeed capable of isolated involvement in any sin. However, habitual sin is inconsistent with salvation. We do not know God's definition of the practice of sin. Therefore, these warnings end up primarily being a personal warning to people in long-term sins. They should examine themselves to consider whether they really believe in Christ (2 Cor. 13:5). Relative to evaluating others, a categorical denial of another's salvation should not be made on their behavior alone if they profess faith. However, a working assumption can be made that a person in lasting sin might not be a genuine believer. In such cases a Christian worker should repeat the gospel of grace. The issue in the above text is not loss of salvation. It concerns practical evidence that a person has never possessed salvation.

### 1 Corinthians 9:24-27

- Do you not know that those who run in a race all run, but only one receives the prize? Run in such a way that you may win. And everyone who competes in the games exercises self-control in all things. They then do it to receive a perishable wreath, but we an imperishable. Therefore I run in such a way, as not without aim; I box in such a way, as not beating the air; but I buffet my body and make it my slave, lest possibly, after I have preached to others, I myself should be disqualified [1 Cor. 9:24-27].

Paul's subject here cannot be salvation. Salvation does not come through human work. The athletic imagery involves rewards for the believer at the Judgment Seat of Christ. Mention of disqualification in v. 27 is not the loss of salvation. Paul is concerned about being disqualified from ministry due to sin. He works hard so as to not be disqualified from gaining a full reward (possible references to loss of rewards Col. 2:18; 2 John 8; Rev. 3:11).

## 1 Corinthians 11:28-32

- But let a man examine himself, and so let him eat of the bread and drink of the cup. For he who eats and drinks, eats and drinks judgment to himself, if he does not judge the body right. But when we are judged, we are disciplined by the Lord in order that we may not be condemned along with the world (1 Cor: 11:28,32).

There need be no confusion over this communion text. Perhaps the King James translation of "damnation" in v. 29 is the source of the problem. However, the warning to Corinthian believers is of a judgment that is clearly distinguished from the condemnation which the world receives. The danger is not eternal condemnation but rather of temporal chastisement such as weakness, sickness, or physical death (v. 30).

## 1 Corinthians 15:1-2; Col. 1:21-23 [10]

- [b]y which also you are saved, if you hold fast the word which I reached to you, unless you believed in vain [1 Cor. 15:2].

- [i]f indeed you continue in the faith firmly established and steadfast, and not moved away from the hope of the gospel that you

---

[10] It is difficult to know whether to include Luke 9:62 in this classification. Jesus is probably saying the disciple who "looks back" is especially unworthy of God's grace and blessings, but He is not saying he has no salvation. Such a person is unfit for ministry. However, if the subject is salvation not Christian living, then Luke 9:62 teaches one who repudiates Christ never had saving faith as in the line of reasoning given above (1 Cor. 15:1-2 and Col. 1:21-23). A person who visibly follows Jesus and/or even participates in Christian work but falls back to a former repudiation of the cross possesses at best intellectual faith or emotional faith but never trusted Jesus. (See *Not By Bread Alone; An Outlined Guide to Bible Doctrine*, p.133, for explanation of intellectual or emotional faith).

have heard, which was proclaimed in all creation under heaven, and of which I, Paul, was made a minister [ Col. 1:23].

Biblical calls to continue in the faith are quite consistent with the security of believers. God uses such Scriptural commands to keep believers in the faith and thereby keep them in salvation.

Those with genuine faith might have doubts, or disobey, or even occasionally verbally deny Christianity to others, but genuine believers do not sincerely repudiate the deity, resurrection, or blood of Christ within their own hearts or to God the Father. Jesus says in John 10:4b-5 "the sheep follow him because they know his voice. And a stranger they simply will not follow, but will flee from him, because they do not know the voice of strangers." 1 John 2:19 teaches that those who renounce Christ and His cross **never were saved in the first place**. "They went out from us, but they were not really of us, for if they had been of us, they would have remained with us, but they went out in order that it might be shown that they all are not of us." Genuine believers always believe. Though salvation is a past tense matter (e.g., Eph. 2:8,9; Titus 3:5, both past tense in the Greek), faith in the Bible is often in the present tense (e.g., John 3:16, …"that whoever believes in Him might not perish…"). Genuine believers always believe because God keeps them in the faith.

• Now to Him who is able **to keep** you from

stumbling, and to make you stand in the
presence of His glory blameless with great
joy [Jude v.24].

- [t]o obtain an inheritance which is imperishable and undefiled and will not fade
  away, reserved in heaven for you, who are
  **protected** by the power of God through
  faith for a salvation ready to be revealed in
  the last time [1 Peter 1:4-5].[11]

Warnings in the Bible to "keep the faith" are not
inconsistent with thinking true believers in fact will
keep the faith. One of the ways God keeps believers
in the faith is through Biblical commands and warnings. For those with genuine faith the commands to
continue help ensure continuance. Also, such commands warn unbelievers within the visible church.

---

[11] Peter does not explain whether faith in 1 Pet. 1:5 refers to a
past faith, i.e. initial saving faith, or an ongoing faith in the present. Those who adhere to eternal security usually see the faith in
v. 5 as a past initial act of faith. Initial faith in Christ brings
God's protection and causes a reservation in heaven. On the other
hand, Arminians naturally see faith in v. 5 as ongoing faith. So
long as a person has ongoing faith, he has God's protection of
salvation as reservation in heaven. In all fairness, salvation in 1
Pet. 1:5 refers to a future salvation from sin's presence, not a past
salvation from sin's penalty. Therefore, faith in v. 5 need not
refer to a past act of initial faith in Christ but rather ongoing faith
in the Christian life. One who comes to 1 Pet. 1:4-5 already believing in eternal security can agree with Arminians that faith
refers to ongoing faith. However, there is no doubt that a believer
will continue to believe. **1 Pet. 1:4-5 probably means God's
power protects believers by keeping them in faith.**

There is a need for ministers to follow Paul's example of warning to continue. "Examine yourselves to see if you are in the faith" (2 Cor. 13:5). Some who think they have saving faith really have only intellectual or emotional faith (see *Not By Bread Alone; An Outlined Guide to Bible Doctrine, p.133*). Paul's warning in 1 Cor. 15:1-2 and Col. 1:21-23 are concerns that some in New Testament churches lacked trust in Christ. Any other definition of faith than trust constitutes a vain faith that will not last. Thus, Paul's warnings do not concern believers who might lose salvation, but those whose concept of faith does not involve trust (dependence, reliance) in Christ, God the Son, who died and rose again. These would not lose salvation. Instead, they do not have salvation because they lack the kind of faith that saves.

## Galatians 5:1-4

- It was for freedom that Christ set us free; therefore keep standing firm and do not be subject again to a yoke of slavery. Behold I, Paul, say to you that if you receive circumcision, Christ will be of no benefit to you....You have been severed from Christ, you who are seeking to be justified by law; you have fallen from grace [Gal. 5:1-2,4].

### *Law versus Grace*

The debate in the book of Galatians concerns the choice between Law and Grace. Are people saved by Law-keeping (either the Law of Moses or other systems of laws) or are they saved by grace? Paul in Galatians argues for the doctrine of grace not Law (e.g. 2:16, 3:11, etc.). Pages of verses can be quoted that salvation does not come through good works (see Rom. 4:5; Eph. 2:9; Titus 3:5). It is inexcusable to add works to faith as a requirement for salvation. However, some Christians from New Testament days to the present have been confused. Many try to merge faith and works. **Faith alone saves**. Works add nothing. When a person trusts in good works or religious rituals, he is definitely unsaved; but how shall we evaluate the spiritual status of one who mixes faith and works, grace and Law? Heresy is confusing. It is wrong to trust in both Christ and Law-keeping for salvation, but many adopt such false thinking.

Likely, millions are really trusting in their own goodness or in their religion without any real faith in Christ and the cross. These are unsaved despite their associations with Christian organizations and rituals.

Nevertheless, Acts 15:5 refers to the "Pharisees who had **believed**" insisting that circumcision and Law-keeping were also essential for salvation. Therefore, it seems possible for genuine Christians to become confused over the conditions for salvation. Even believers can be led astray by false teaching. Paul's writings in the book of Galatians show his concern that saved people can **fall away from the true doctrine of grace.** Those who insist upon Law-keeping for salvation might be saved, or they might be unsaved (false brethren Gal. 2:4). Perhaps only

God knows whether those with such false ideas have faith in Christ (2 Tim. 2:19). God can tell when one is really trusting his own goodness or trusting a church to save. God can also determine whether some have weak faith in the cross even when they also needlessly do more to guarantee salvation because they lack assurance. They are saved but add works to faith as a means of being extra certain to obtain salvation. They keep the Law as an extra measure of precaution. No doubt some with such weak faith will actually be surprised to find they had salvation through grace alone and endured much needless anxiety in this life. While Galatians has a strong message for unbelievers who base salvation on their own goodness, the original recipients were already saved. In Galatians 5 Paul urges them to continue their lives in freedom from the Law. He wants them to continue in grace theology and in a Christian way of life based upon grace theology, not to fall away from grace doctrines and a grace-oriented Christian life.

## *No benefit in this life (Gal. 5:2)*

What happens to believers who trust in the Lord Jesus but then add the idea they should also keep the Law (the Law of Moses or other forms of laws) to either earn or keep salvation?

Paul should not be understood as warning the Galatians they would lose salvation. Yet, by adopting a mixture of law and grace they would **lose all the**

**benefits of Christ as it pertains to this life**. Believers who abandon the doctrine of grace do not lose eternal life, but they do lose truths that are absolutely necessary to living the Christian life. **Works theology inevitably leads to lack of assurance.** Fear, not gratitude, becomes the motivation for work. As opposed to enjoyment of God's unconditional love and grace, a believer who thinks salvation is in doubt without additional works cannot have the benefits of true Christianity. Christ does not operate through a system of Law. Therefore, in a sense it is not even possible to live a Christian life by mixing Law and grace. Believers who try to add Law to grace are not really living a Christian life as taught in the New Testament. When Paul says in Gal. 5:2 that those who mix Law and grace lose the benefit of Christ, he does not mean they lose eternal life. He does mean they lose all benefits of the Christian life in this world. Galatians 5:4 also gives the strongest type of warning to believers (the Galatians were believers, 5:1) who are in danger of falling away from the doctrine of grace.

### Severed from Christ (Gal. 5:4)

The phrase "fallen from grace" in Gal. 5:4 does not refer to a loss of salvation. Those who place themselves back under a yoke of the Law **fall away from the doctrine of grace** and from the outlook and relationship to Christ based on a system of grace. Being "severed from Christ" means those who **fall from grace theology and the Christian life arising**

**from it are cut off from fellowship with Christ**. To abandon the real way of Christian living for an unscriptural way that God will not use means being **severed from opportunities for Christian growth and service**. A person can still be saved though he attempts to add works to grace. However, he cannot really experience Christian living. Also, those with such false doctrines are **totally unqualified to minister to others**. It is the theological equivalent to "malpractice." They harm others spiritually by their error. In addition to being **severed from fellowship and genuine ministry**, they are **severed from Christian growth and activity**. Christ and the Spirit of Christ operate by grace, not law. Those who add works to faith cut themselves off from the only way Christ wants to lead them.

## *Conclusion on Galatians 5:1-4*

The warnings of Galatians 5:1-4 can be interpreted as consistent with eternal security. Paul does not threaten a loss of eternal life. However, his words are as harsh as possible without implying an eternity in hell. Believers who get mixed up ideas that salvation requires Law-keeping lose all the benefits of Christ relative to living real Christianity (v. 2). To fall away from the doctrine of grace and the way of Christian living arising from it is to be cut off from fellowship to Christ (v. 4). Since the truths about God's grace are essential to Biblical Christian living, believers who disagree are cut off in terms of potential for growth and ministry (v. 4). Believers who misunderstand grace do not lose salvation, but they do lose the foundation for Christian living. The extreme consequences explain Paul's deep concern for the Galatians.

## 2 Tim. 2:12b

- ...if we deny Him, He will also deny us...[2 Tim. 2:12b].

In the context, Paul has told Timothy to "be strong" (v. 1) and to "suffer hardship" (v. 3). Then he gives examples of disciplined lives, a soldier (v. 4) an athlete (v. 5), and a farmer (v. 6).

The statement in 2 Tim: 2:12b is part of an early Christian hymn. While the specific interpretation in each phrase can be difficult, the overall hymn teaches the merits of dedication and discipline.

If "we" is restricted to saved people, then the phrase can mean those who are ashamed to admit they are believers (see 2 Tim. 1:8) will be denied the full rewards God wanted to give them. This would not be a loss of salvation but a loss of crowns, higher positions in the Kingdom, or a deeper glory in the resurrection body (see 1 Cor. 3:15; Col. 2:18; 1 John 2:28; 2 John 8; Rev. 3:11 for verses that might speak of a believer's rewards at the Judgment Seat of Christ). Actually, the very next statement is perhaps an assertion that a believer's salvation is secure even if he or she is denied full rewards. **"If we are faithless, He remains faithful...(2 Tim. 2:13a).**

If the "we" in 2 Tim. 2:12b is not restricted to believers and involves people in general, another interpretation results. Those who deny Christ as Savior in this life, i.e., they will not believe on Him, will be denied by the Lord in the future judgment (see Matt. 7:22-23). Then the next verse (v. 13) would mean those who are faithless (unbelievers) will face eternal punishment. God will be faithful in His own justice and His warnings of destruction.

The first view fits a context that calls for believers to endure hardship. We will be denied rewards if we disobey. However, the second view also fits the subject in vv. 9-10 (enduring hardship so that the elect obtain salvation and eternal glory). Perhaps 2 Tim. 2:11-12a refers to the saved who obtain life and also rewards. 2 Tim. 12b-13 would then refer to those who deny Christ as Savior and are faithless (unbelievers). These will forfeit eternal glory and be denied salvation. By either way of understanding the phrase, it is compatible with he doctrine that a believer does not lose salvation.

### Warning passages from Hebrews

The author of Hebrews gives five warning passages in his book: 2:1-4; 3:6 – 4:11 (especially 3:6, 12, 14, 4:11); 6:4-8; 10:26-31; 12:25-29. Those who deny eternal security point to Hebrews 6:4-6 or 10:26-31 as strong evidences for their position. However, all these texts can be better understood in ways compatible with eternal security. Before explaining

them, it will be necessary to give an opinion about
the original recipients to Hebrews. Were the readers
a mixture of saved and unsaved Jews? If so, the
warning passages can be read as warnings to the
unsaved about placing faith in Christ before the fires
of hell. If the original readers are strictly believers,
then the warnings urge them to avoid the fires of
chastisement.[12] Instead of neglecting eternity, believers must work toward obtaining a full reward and
share in Christ's coming Kingdom. The exact interpretation of the warning passages depends upon
whether one views the recipients as unsaved (evangelistic warnings) or saved (warnings about being
unfaithful). However, both options can lead to interpretations consistent with eternal security. After
dealing with the identity of the original readers, there
will be a study on each warning passage.

### *The original readers of Hebrews*

The recipients of Hebrews are obviously Jewish.
They have affiliated with Christian circles but are
being urged to return to Judaism.[13] The author warns
against this choice. Obviously, a local church can
have members who are unsaved. Could these warnings be directed at unbelievers in Hebrew churches?

---

[12] Fire would be an agricultural metaphor speaking of purging a
field from impurity and/or a fire that burns away worthless work
as a believer forfeits rewards (1 Cor. 3:15).

[13] We need not concern ourselves here whether the readers are
being pulled back to mainstream Judaism or a Jewish splinter
sect.

They would then be evangelistic warnings urging faith in Christ. The other option is that the warnings are directed at genuine believers. They urge believers not to forsake the visible church and return to associations with the synagogue. By an evil choice, they would endure the fires of God's chastisement (hardship in this life but not hell) and loss of full rewards in heaven. Which view is best?

The choice is admittedly difficult. Nevertheless, this writer prefers to take the warning texts in Hebrews as directed to believers. The definition of *salvation* in Hebrews gives a slight favor to the idea that these warnings are directed at those already saved. What does the author of Hebrews mean by *salvation*? In the Bible there is a past tense salvation. A believer has already been saved (past tense) from the penalty of sin. If Hebrews intends this definition of salvation, then the warning texts are evangelistic. Nevertheless, the Bible also refers to a future aspect to salvation even for those already saved from sin's penalty. In the future believers will be saved from sin's presence (Rom. 13:11). Christ's future deliverance (salvation) includes all the blessings from His Second Coming (binding the devil, a resurrection body for the church saints, rewards, and positions of authority in the Kingdom). Although all believers will be in heaven, there will be various levels of rewards (crowns), various positions of authority in sharing Christ's rule (Luke 19:17, 19) and even different levels of glory among resurrection bodies (1 Cor. 15:41-42). While no Christian loses admission to heaven, there will be degrees of sharing in the Kingdom. If we take *salvation* in Hebrews to refer to a future deliverance at Christ's coming, then the warning passages apply to believers. They would be warnings about neglecting to live for eternity. Faithlessness will result in a diminished share in the blessings of the future salvation.

Hebrews definitely gives a future outlook; (1) "heir of all things" 1:2, (2) "He **again** brings the firstborn into the world" 1:6, i.e., the Second Coming, (3) "the world to come" 2:5, (4) "bringing many sons to glory" 2:10, (5) "heavenly calling" 3:1, (6) "the age to come" 6:5, (7) "the day drawing near" 10:25. Even more important, several usages of the term *salvation* show that the author defines it as a future deliverance from sin's presence and curse (not just salvation in the past from sin's penalty).

- Are they not all ministering spirits, sent out to render service for the sake of those who **will inherit salvation** [Heb. 1:14].

- [s]o Christ also, having been offered once to bear the sins of many, shall appear **a second time for salvation** without reference to sin, to those who eagerly await Him [Heb. 9:28].

The position that takes the warnings in Hebrews as evangelistic warnings to unbelievers about salvation from sin's penalty is a valid position. It preserves the doctrine of eternal security. However, Hebrews probably gives warnings to Christians about missing the full blessings of future salvation. Believers must not live only for this life, neglecting the Lord's return. If so, they could very well miss out on some aspects to future deliverance (salvation). Believers have already been saved from sin's penalty, but can still miss their full potential for rewards and blessings in the future salvation Christ will bring. An illustration about an earthly inheritance should help clarify Hebrew's perspective about our heavenly inheritance. Suppose a man has the potential to obtain a staggering inheritance. The degree to which he could share in the future is beyond understanding. He stands to inherit a blessing greater than anyone in world history. However, suppose through neglect of his benefactor he receives only a small fraction of what he could have inherited. He still obtained a huge benefit. From one point of view he did not miss out on the inheritance. Nevertheless, from another perspective the loss of the potential full inheritance could be viewed as missing out on his inheritance. By neglect he lost out on what he could have possessed.

The Lord will return to bring a complete salvation to this world. There will be salvation from sin's presence (and the curse). All believers have already been eternally saved from sin's penalty. Yet, there will be various degrees of sharing in the future salvation. No believer will miss out totally. Still, through unfaith-

fulness and neglect of living with Christ's future rescue in view, many believers will miss the full inheritance that they could otherwise have obtained. All
will share in the future deliverance the Lord brings at
His Second Coming, but many will miss the full
blessing of this salvation. This will be such a huge
loss of what they could have possessed, it can be
conceived as a loss of the deepest share in salvation.
It is not that a believer can go to hell or miss out on
entrance into heaven, but a believer can miss out on
the full blessings of Christ's future deliverance (rewards, position in the Kingdom, degrees of glory in
the resurrection body, etc.). Hebrews probably warns
believers against neglecting to live now in ways that
obtain a deeper reward in the salvation that is coming. Hebrews probably warns about the fire of chastisement during this life and the loss of rewards.

Now we shall address each warning passage. The
first view will give an interpretation based on the
assumption the warning is evangelistic (directed at
unbelievers). The second view will give an interpretation that results from the assumption that the warning is for believers. Regardless of the exact view
adopted, **the main truth must not be lost**. **There
are ways of handling Hebrews that are consistent
with eternal security.**

### *The first warning passage, Hebrews 2:1-4*

- ...[H]ow shall we escape if we neglect so
great a salvation? After it was at the first

spoken through the Lord, it was confirmed
to us by those who heard [Heb. 2:3a].

## As addressed to the unsaved among the Hebrews

Those who believe the original readers included
some unsaved will view this warning as evangelistic.
Pay attention to the gospel (Heb. 2:1a). Do not drift
through life neglecting the invitation to faith in
Christ (Heb. 2:1b). Those who disobeyed the law
obtained punishment (v. 2). Those who neglect salvation (from sin's penalty) offered through faith in
Christ will not escape eternal punishment (v. 3).

## As addressed to believers

Those who think Hebrews speaks only to believers will see this as a warning to live for eternity. Salvation refers to a future rescue through the Lord's
Second Coming. There will be a future deliverance
from this evil world system and from all aspects of
the curse (such as sickness and physical death). This
future salvation also includes rewards and positions
of authority in the millennial Kingdom and eternity.
Christians must pay close attention to what the Lord
taught about His future deliverance (i.e. a future salvation, see Heb. 2:1a). If we want to share a deeper
degree of reward, blessings, and authority in these
future aspects of salvation, we cannot just drift
through life now (see Heb. 2:1b). Some believers are
lazy and apathetic about their level of reward and
authority in the future Kingdom. They are careless
concerning what they have learned about the future

rescue (salvation) from the presence of sin and from this world system. Believers who live only for this present time neglecting Christ's teaching about His future salvation will receive chastisement now and loss of rewards later (v. 2, just recompense). Those who pay attention to what Christ taught about the future will not just drift through this life. They will not neglect the future salvation that is coming with degrees of sharing in rewards, positions in the Kingdom, and the glory of the resurrection body. They will live now so as to obtain the fullest possible share when Christ comes to save us out of and from this sinful and transitory world.[14] They will take action in this world that will be of benefit in "the world to come" (v. 5).

Viewing salvation from a future angle probably seems unusual to Christians who read the Bible today. Our thinking emphasizes salvation from sin's penalty. However, the warning in Heb. 2:1-4 is sandwiched between two references to future salvation. Hebrews 1:14 clearly uses salvation to encompass all future blessings. Also, Heb. 2:5 is tied to the arguments of 2:1-4. Heb. 2:5 tells of the "world to come." While living in this world believers must pay attention to how they can obtain a larger reward and a deeper share in the rule, power, and glory of the

---

[14] The Lord will save believers **out of** this world at the Rapture. This is also a salvation from the suffering, persecution, and temptation **from** the world (i.e. caused by living in a world dominated by Satan and a world system opposed to Christ).

world to come.

### Conclusion

The first warning passage is not teaching that believers can lose salvation from sin's penalty by drifting away or neglect. We have given two alternative interpretations. The above section reveals the author's preference for one view over another. However, both interpretations supply the need for an understanding of Hebrews 2:1-4 that is compatible with eternal security.

*The second warning passage, Hebrews, Chapters 3-4*

- [B]ut Christ was faithful as a Son over His house whose house we are, if we hold fast our confidence and the boast of our hope firm until the end [Heb. 3:6].

- Take care, brethren, lest there should be any one of you an evil, unbelieving heart, in falling away from the living God [Heb. 3:12].

- For we have become partakers of Christ, if we hold fast the beginning of our assurance firm until the end [Heb 3:14].

- Let us therefore be diligent to enter that rest, lest anyone fall through following the same example of disobedience...[Heb. 4:11].

As addressed to the unsaved among the Hebrews

One earlier conclusion from this study is that
genuine saving faith keeps faith. God keeps a believer believing. A person who trusts Christ as Savior
will not renounce the deity, blood, or resurrection of
Christ (see previous material on pages 44-47 above
that deals with 1 Cor. 15:1-2). The type of faith that
saves (trust) leads to an ongoing faith. Other types of
faith such as intellectual faith in certain facts about
God (James 2:19) or emotional faith that Jesus can
save from temporal difficulties (without an interest in
salvation from sin, e.g. Luke 8:13) do not save. The
warnings in Hebrews 3-4 may be addressed to unbelievers who have associated with Jewish churches.
These do not possess the type of faith that saves and
that lasts (holds fast). By this understanding "house"
in Heb. 3:6 refers to being part of God's family, and
"partaker" in Heb. 3:14 refers to saving union with
Christ. Heb. 3:6 is a warning to examine whether
some among the readers might not have saving faith
(the kind that continues to believe). Heb. 3:12 warns
against being an unbeliever who falls away from
God. They would fall away by rejecting God's ap-
peals to trust Jesus. The Hebrew readers are being
invited to leave the church and return to the synagogue. Again, in Heb. 3:14 the author may be urging
the readers to make sure they have personal faith in
Christ. (**Personal** in the sense of **trust** not just intellectual faith in facts about Jesus or emotional faith
that He can help with temporal problems). The type
of faith that saves keeps believing. Other definitions
of faith do not involve saving faith. The author is not

worried that a believer has lost salvation. He is worried that some readers, though joined to a church, might not have ever trusted in Christ. Heb. 4:11 becomes another evangelistic appeal to enter salvation by resting through faith in Christ and resting from works as a way of earning salvation (4:10).

### As addressed to believers

The warnings in Hebrews 3-4 can also be understood as warnings to believers to remain active in worship/service, to keep working in an active partnership with Christ, and to enter a full inheritance (reward). Remember the Hebrews are struggling with the temptation to forsake the visible church and return to association with Judaism. The "houses" in Hebrews 3 do not seem to refer to the family of God. Moses' house in Heb. 3:5 refers to the worship/service system in the tabernacle. Only priests could serve in the "house of God" as limited to the priestly functions within the holy place and holy of holies. One could still be saved without active participation in God's house (the place and system of priests). Christ's house in v. 6 probably also refers to active participation in priestly worship. Unlike the Law where only a minority could be priests, all believers under the New Testament (covenant) have standing as priests with God; but some withdraw from involvement in the activity of worship and service. Christians can never drop out of the family of God, but they can refuse to participate in God's system of worship and service. They can remove themselves from God's house by refusing to assemble with other believer-priests as they worship. The familiar call to assemble in Hebrews 10:25 is preceded by a statement in Heb. 10:21 that Christ is the great priest over the house of God. Thus, the command not to forsake church equals a warning to remain in God's house. Hebrews 3:6 is probably a warning for Jewish believers not to drop out of God's house (not a church building but the assembly of believer-priests as they worship) and return to the synagogue.[15] A person can be saved and part of God's family but depart from involvement with the church, the house of worship. Heb. 3:6 encourages remaining active in "Christ's house."

Assuming the author addresses the saved, Heb. 3:12 would be referring to the ongoing faith of Christian living. A saved person has believed in the cross but must constantly believe the commands and teaching of the Bible. It would exhibit a great lack of faith for a Jewish Christian to forsake the church out of social pressures and return to associations with Juda-

---

[15] Moses' house in Heb. 3:5 refers to the tabernacle (the house of God) with its holy place and also refers to the function of the Old Testament priesthood that offered worship and service in that place. The definition of house in Heb. 3:6 includes both the **place** of worship and also the **participants** (priests in their role of worship and service). Christ's house is the heavenly tabernacle (heaven) and its holy **place** (the presence of God on His throne) with a New Testament **priesthood** of worship and service to God. A believer always has the position as a priest but can drop away from the functions of service and worship.

ism. Leaving the church might not cause a loss of salvation but it does break fellowship with God and can be called "falling away from the living God" (v. 12).

Heb. 3:14 can be taken as a warning totally restricted to believers. Perhaps understanding *partakers* as a saving union with Christ misses the intent of the warning. Luke 5:7 uses the same Greek word of business partners in a joint fishing business. The definition of "partners" or "co-laborers" also fits the usage in Heb. 1:9 ("companions," NASB) and 3:1 ("partners in the heavenly calling or heavenly work"). The stress need not be on spiritual union but upon active participation as co-laborers with Christ in the work of ministry. Just as the concept of the "house" in v. 6 warns of dropping out of activity in God's system of worship, so v. 14 warns against failing to be a working partner with Christ in service. Believers who are active partners with Christ's work in this world will share in a more full partnership in His power and glory later. We must both remain in Christ's house of worship (the church) and remain active partners with Him to realize full potential for inheritance.

If addressed to believers, Heb. 4:11 is a command to diligently strive for the fullest possible inheritance. The concept of rest may not seem to have anything to do with inheritance until we realize the context and the Jewish way of thinking. For them *rest* is closely linked with inheritance. After God **rested** from His creative work, He could **enjoy the inheritance** He had made for Himself. Those in the Exodus generation were called to conquer the Promised Land. Then they could enter the **rest** and **enjoy the inheritance**. Notice the connection between rest and inheritance in Deut. 3:18-20 and 12:9-11.

- [f]or you have not yet come to the **resting** place and the **inheritance** which the LORD your God is giving you. When you cross the Jordan and live in the land which the LORD your God is giving you to **inherit**, and He gives you **rest** from all your enemies around you so that you live in security… [Deut. 12:9-10].

The author of Hebrews teaches that not even Joshua led God's people to full rest and inheritance in the land (Heb. 4:8). The greatest rest and inheritance still lies in the future. Believers have not yet entered rest from labor. Now is the time to work. Rest and inheritance are coming.

Someday we will cease earth's labors (at death or the Rapture). However, the present is not a time of rest but rather labor, even warfare as implied by the Old Testament parallels of fighting to obtain full inheritance in the Promised Land. Heb. 4:11 is certainly not an appeal to earn salvation from hell by diligent work. The command in Heb. 4:11 tells believers to be diligent to enter the inheritance God wants to give them. The author's definition of "inheritance" is not just minimal deliverance from eternal punishment but the full possession of rewards and blessings that God wants bestowed. When strictly defined as a full possession or inheritance, it is possible to miss out on the inheritance God wants to give and obtain only a rescue from damnation. This is a huge blessing but not the full inheritance that can be possessed by diligence. All believers will enter eternal rest in the common meaning of that phrase, rest from earthly troubles. Yet, some will inherit more rewards and blessings than others will. All believers will be citizens and residents of God's Kingdom, but many will miss the (complete) inheritance God wanted to give them. Just as many in the Exodus generations were saved but did not obtain their inheritance in the Promised Land, so believers can be saved from hell but miss the full inheritance God wants to give. Just as believers in Joshua's generation were saved from hell but did not obtain the full inheritance God wanted to give, there is a danger of a believer going to heaven but missing the full inheritance God wanted to give. If "inheritance" is viewed as the potential for the greatest possible blessing, it is possible for a believer to miss out on the promised rest by a lack of diligence. Heb. 4:11 warns to obey and work now to enter full inheritance and rest in the future.

All the warnings in Hebrews 3-4 can be taken as warnings to believers without implying a loss of salvation from eternal punishment: (1) "Remain in

God's house" (Heb. 3:6), i.e., remain in the church assembly as a system of priestly worship and service. (2) "Do not fall away from fellowship with the living God by returning to ties with Judaism" (Heb. 3:12). (3) "Keep your partnership in working for Christ" (Heb. 3:14). (4) "Do not rest yet. Be diligent and obedient so you do not miss out on any part of the rest (the complete inheritance) God wants to give you" (Heb. 4:11). Believing Hebrews would not lose salvation by dropping out of the church. However, they could withdraw from God's house Heb. 3:6 (system of worship). They could fall away from fellowship with God (Heb. 3:12). They could cease to be active partners in Christ's work (Heb. 3:14). Like the Hebrews of Old Testament days (many of whom were also saved), they could fail to enter the inheritance (rest) God wanted to give them (Heb. 4:11). They would have salvation from hell, but God wanted to give more. If they forsake the church and return outwardly to Judaism, they will miss the rest (inheritance) God wanted them to have (but not miss heaven itself).

### Conclusion

The second warning passage may urge unbelievers affiliated with the church to come to faith in Christ. It may urge believers to remain diligent and involved to obtain the complete inheritance God wants for them. It does not contradict the basic doctrines of Scripture that teach the eternal security of the believer.

## *The third warning passage, Hebrews 6:1-12*

- For in the case of those who have once been enlightened and have tasted of the heavenly gift and have been made partakers of the Holy Spirit, and have tasted the good word of God and the powers of the age to come, and then have fallen away, it is impossible to renew them again to repentance, since they again crucify to themselves the Son of God, and put Him to open shame. For ground that drinks the rain which often falls upon it and brings forth vegetation useful to those for whose sake it is also tilled, receives a blessing from God; but if it yields thorns and thistles, it is worthless and close to being cursed, and it ends up being burned [Heb. 6:4-8].

If a person comes to this text already thinking believers can forfeit salvation, he will interpret these verses as confirmation. However, assuming this is the correct view, then Hebrews 6:6 would be teaching **once lost always lost**. It says that for those who fall away "it is impossible to renew them again to repentance." The true interpretation of Hebrews 6:1-12 lies in another direction. Again, the precise outcome depends on whether one thinks the author directs his warning at unsaved people associated with the visible church or strictly believers. If the words are to unbelievers, this is a warning to place faith in Christ. They must press on to maturity, i.e., out of

Judaism to full Christianity (v. 1). If not, then the
curse and burning of v. 8 would be a reference to
hell. On the other hand, this warning could be aimed
at believers. Then the burning of v. 8 would be a
metaphor for burning a field to remove impurities
(weeds) and produce fertility. Notice the actual figure employed is of a field. Burning would refer to
God's chastisement of a believer in this life and perhaps the loss of rewards at the Judgment Seat of
Christ (1 Cor. 3:15). While the precise interpretation
varies depending on the conclusion about the recipients, **in neither case does Hebrews 6 need to be
understood as dealing with Christians who lose
salvation.** Now we will look at the passage in detail.

### As addressed to unbelievers

Suppose the author directs his warnings to unbelievers who assemble within the Hebrew churches.
Leaving elemental teaching and pressing on to maturity would be a call to leave permanently all forms of
Judaism and enter by faith into God's more advanced
system, Christianity. It might not be possible for this
to happen. The impossible renewal of v. 6 may mean
that some of the Hebrews have rejected Christ to the
point of no return, or maybe this means nothing further the author can say or do will produce saving repentance. However, God can change hearts (v. 3).
The strongest evidence for thinking unsaved people
are in view comes from the phrase in v. 6 "crucify to
themselves the Son of God" and v. 9 "things that accompany salvation." If a person actually believes

Jesus was a false messiah who deserved to die, he is indeed unsaved. Also, by saying he expected better things of the readers, "things that accompany salvation" maybe the author implies his previous words describe the unsaved. Maybe the picture in vv. 4-6 refers to persons who have been exposed to Christian people and truths but have not placed faith in Christ. In current language we would call them "seekers." They are considering faith in Christ. They have moved away from Judaism but not yet to Christian faith. They have some truths about the Lord Jesus (enlightenment v. 4). They have had some experience of what salvation means because they associated with the saved (tasting or sampling the heavenly gift of salvation, v. 4). They have had some participation with the Holy Spirit's convicting ministry (partakers v. 4). They have sampled (tasted) the blessings of the Scripture and had seen miracles (v. 5). However, there was pressure upon those Jewish people to fall away from the church and thereby reject any further influence to the possibility of faith in Christ. If they return to the conclusion that Jesus was a false christ who deserved death (crucify to themselves the Son of God v. 6), they might experience blindness and reprobation. At the very least nothing the author could do would ever change their minds (i.e., renew repentance v. 6). God alone could change this serious falling away (v. 3), but unless reversed the end would be burning (v. 8). Heb. 6:1-8 can be interpreted as a warning for unbelievers (seekers) to come to faith in Christ and not return to Judaism. The result squares with eternal security. Another option would be the idea that the warning is for believers with the fire of v. 8 being severe chastisement for falling away from the church.

### As addressed to believers

The descriptions "again crucify to themselves the Son of God" (v. 6) and "things that accompany salvation" need not rule out the view that Hebrews 6 is addressed to those already saved. Suppose the description of "crucify Christ" does not speak of a deliberately expressed theological position. Instead, it might be an inadvertent, unconscious, and unintended description of one who falls away (*forsake* - 10:25) from the church and returns to associations with Judaism. The description "crucify Christ" might not give a true heart-felt theological conviction but rather a sociological behavior. Anyone who fell away from a Christian assembly to listen to false teachers from a Judaistic cult sided with Christ's killers by actions and associations without realizing it. A genuine Christian who falls away from the church can side with Christ's enemies by association. The author would not be classifying the readers as unsaved. He would be using guilt by association tactic. In theological beliefs they had not agreed with the crucifixion, but by affiliation with Christ's enemies their actions are inconsistent with their beliefs. Christians must not return to the religious circles that killed Christ. If they drop out of the church and return to involvement in Judaism, they would be assisting the very group whose leaders wanted Jesus killed as a false messiah. Most likely the Hebrew readers never realized the true picture of what it would mean to fall away from Christian circles and a return to their old friends in Judaism. Perhaps they thought it would be a simple innocent change. The author wants them to see that even without intent and without realization those who forsook the church for a return to Judaism would be siding (in association but not belief) with those who killed Jesus as a false messiah. Dropping fellowship with the church might be a more serious matter and might make God angrier than the Hebrew believers ever realized. If the phrase (crucifying the Son of God) is interpreted as sociological behavior and not theological belief, it can still refer to genuine Christians.

Likewise, the phrase "things that accompany salvation" (v. 9) need not imply the readers are unbelievers. Salvation in the book of Hebrews has a future tense emphasis. Christ will return to save believers both out of and from this world and from the curse of sin. This deliverance involves degrees of rewards, co-ruling with Christ in various ranks of authority, and levels of glory in the resurrection body. All will have a share in this future type of salvation. Some will have a greater and more glorious degree of sharing than others. Jewish believers who fell away from the church for a return to Judaism could still be saved from sin's penalty in eternal hell. However, they would miss out on the deepest bless-

ing of future salvation upon the Lord's return.
"Things that accompany salvation" in v. 9 equals
"pressing on to maturity" in vv. 1-3. It also equals the
description in vv. 11-12. In Heb. 6:11-12 the author
calls for diligence and not sluggishness. The outcome
will be the realization of the full hope for believers.
With faith and endurance in this life believers can
have the full inheritance and full realization of all
promises about the future deliverance (salvation) at
the Lord's return. The issue is not whether believers
are saved from hell and go to heaven. The issue is
whether the saved readers will fall away from the
church and miss out on the full rewards of the future
aspects of salvation.

The phrases, which seem to prove Hebrews 6 concerns unbelievers can also fit believers. A saved Jew
could not crucify Christ in the sense of theological
beliefs, but he could assist Christ's enemies by
falling away from the church and returning to affiliation with Judaism. "Things which accompany salvation" probably refers to a believer pressing on to maturity as he shares the fullest blessings of Christ's
**future salvation** brought at His return. Once those
key phrases can be explained to refer to believers,
other clues can be discovered in Heb. 6:4-6. They
indicate the author writes to believers. The readers
have been "once enlightened." In Heb. 10:32 the author uses "enlightenment" of saving faith. The word
"once" speaks not of the Holy Spirit repeatedly convicting a lost person but of a once-for-all penetration

of blindness that leads to saving faith in Christ. The word "taste" does not mean "sample" in Heb. 2:9 but a full experience. Christ tasted death for every man. We must interpret words by an author's own definition. Therefore, "tasting the heavenly gift" in Hebrews 6:4 refers to a full experience of salvation (the gift) not just an unbeliever indirectly sampling salvation by attending church. It is preferable to see the warning in Heb. 6:4-6 as a warning to saved Jews not to fall away from the church to return to social/religious ties with Judaism. If they do so, it will be impossible for Christian leaders to say or do anything to convince them to repent of their departure (v. 4).[16] Only God could change their minds (v. 3). Such a departure, causing shame to Christ (v. 6) by ties with those who hate Christ, would not leave a believer's relationship with God unaffected. Instead of maturity, they could expect severe chastisement. The picture in vv. 7-8 is not that of eternal hell. It is the picture of a field. The same field yields an abundant crop and blessing from God one season (v. 7), but the next harvest season the same field is worthless relative to fruit (v. 8). It is close to being cursed (but not fully cursed). The farmer burns the weeds and impurities from the field so it can return to a productive season. One can burn thorns and thistles.

---

[16] A good sermon title for Heb. 6:6 would be "What More Can I Say?" The author of Hebrews means he can say and do nothing more to change the minds of his readers if they reject the warning he gives them in the epistle.

One cannot really destroy a field by burning. Such purging actually improves the field. Jewish Christians who fell away from the church towards Judaism rejected the process of maturity. They should not think God will be unconcerned. Instead, He will burn them in the sense of trial and chastisement in this life (but not hell) in order to improve them. The warning does not concern a loss of salvation but of God's anger over believers who ignore maturity and spend their lives in association and friendship with those who hate Christ.

Conclusion

Regardless of the above options as to the exact meaning of Heb. 6:1-12, there is no need to view the statement as a warning that believers can lose salvation from eternal punishment. We have demonstrated valid alternatives to thinking Hebrews 6 contradicts eternal security. Given that the basic doctrines of Scripture support eternal security any view is superior to thinking Hebrews 6 supports Arminianism.

*The fourth warning passage, Hebrews 10:26-31*

- For if we go on sinning willfully after receiving the knowledge of the truth, there no longer remains a sacrifice for sins, but a certain terrifying expectation of judgment, and the fury of a fire which will consume the adversaries. Anyone who has set aside the Law of Moses dies without mercy on the testimony of two or three witnesses.

How much severer punishment do you think he will deserve who has trampled under foot the Son of God, and has regarded as unclean the blood of the covenant by which he was sanctified, and has insulted the Spirit of grace? For we know Him who said, vengeance is mine, I will repay. And again, the Lord will judge his people. It is a terrifying thing to fall into the hands of the living God [Heb. 10:26-31].

Heb. 10:26-31 seems to teach that a Christian can lose salvation. The difficulty can be solved easier than many think. It is important to **interpret first** and **only then apply** a Biblical text. In the rush to make relevant sermons, a minister can bypass careful interpretation. Hebrews is written to readers who are being tempted to return to Judaism (or a splinter Judaistic cult). Heb. 10:26-31 must be interpreted against a background of the transition from Judaism to Christianity.

Those who assert the fourth warning passage concerns a loss of salvation will also have to struggle with the phrase "no more sacrifice for our sins." If Heb. 10:23-31 supports Arminianism, then it also teaches "once lost always lost." Something is wrong with such an interpretation.

### As addressed to unbelievers

One view takes the warning as directed to unbelievers mixed in within the Hebrew church. These "seekers" may have been on the verge of faith in Christ but relatives and friends are also encouraging a return to Judaism. The decision to withdraw from consideration of faith in Christ would lead to a "terrifying expectation of judgment" (Heb 10:27).

Heb. 10:29 seems to refer to unbelievers. If a person believes the Son of God should be trampled, if he thinks Christ's blood is unclean, if he completely insults the convicting work of the Spirit, he is indeed unsaved. Assuming the warning is directed to Jewish unbelievers within the church (Jewish seekers), then the warning of judgment would be warning about hell.

This warning would not involve a believer who loses salvation but a Jewish unbeliever who toys with faith in Christ and even assembles with the church. The deliberate sin of Heb. 10:26 has been defined in v. 25 (forsaking a church for a return to Judaism). "After receiving knowledge of the truth" (the gospel), some decide to keep rejecting the Messiah (i.e. go on willfully sinning), and return to Judaism. The author of Hebrews will not let these think such rejection of Christ and forsaking the influence of the Hebrew church towards faith in the Jewish Savior is only a minor decision. They must not think both views about Jesus are acceptable to God. The willful sin of rejecting Jesus and dropping away from a seeker standing in the church will lead to judgment. If a person knows the truth and willfully sins by rejecting Christ, "there remains no longer a sacrifice for sins" (v. 26). In general this statement warns that the cross is the only answer for sins. The specific meaning, however, lies in verse 18, "there is no longer any offering for sin". The early part of chapter 10 assumes that Old Testament animal sacrifices were only a temporary fix to man's sin (see Heb. 10:4). Christ's one time death is God's complete solution to sin (Heb.10:10,12,14). Now that God offers forgiveness in Christ, He no longer respects animal sacrifice for sin. The precise meaning of the phrase "there is no longer any sacrifice for sin" is that God has set aside animal sacrifice. Jewish people who sin by rejecting the Messiah must not think the animal sacrifices in the temple would be an alternative way of being right with God.

By paying close attention to the argument of the book, we can avoid the mistake of thinking Hebrews 10 teaches a loss of salvation. One alternative is that the author warns Jewish unbelievers who have attended the church assembly and receive the truth about Christ. If they willfully sin by rejecting Him (v. 26) and forsake the truth offered by the church and return to Judaism (v. 25), they must not think God still covers sin through animal sacrifices (v. 26). The choice to refuse faith in Christ and return to Judaism would lead to God's fury, judgment, and vengeance (vv. 29-31).

## As addressed to believers

*An exposition of Heb. 10:26-31:*

Previous material on the warning passages has given evidence they are directed to believers. Heb. 10:26-31 can be interpreted as a warning to Jewish Christians not to drop away from the church and return to involvement with Judaism. Verse 29 supplies the strongest support for thinking of the recipients as unbelievers. By definition a believer in Christ could not agree with the theological positions expressed in v. 29. Yet, in a sociological involvement a believer who helped and encouraged first century Judaism would be in effect supporting the persecution of the Savior and the cross. Without even realizing the full implications, the readers were being influenced to return and support a movement that did "trample under foot the Son of God, regard Christ's blood as unclean, and insult the Holy Spirit's offer of grace" through faith. While a Christian cannot believe such things, believers are quite capable of defection from the true church and giving finances and friendship to groups that despise the Lord Jesus. Those that do so participate in actions and associations contrary to their beliefs. Often they do so inadvertently without thinking. To use the Lord's phrase "they know not what they do." Once we see that Heb. 10:29 could refer to believers, then it is easier to spot additional support for thinking Hebrews 10:26-31 warns genuine Christians as follows:

The readers are sanctified [Heb. 10:10].

The readers are perfected in their standing before God [Heb. 10:14].

The readers are brethren [Heb. 10:19].

The readers should hold fast a confession of hope (i.e. remain with the church v. 25) to give a witness or confession of Christ to their unbelieving Jewish friends [Heb. 10:23].

The author applies the danger to himself by using the pronoun "we." The author of Hebrews is certainly a believer [Heb 10:26].

The fire need not refer to hell [Heb. 10:27]. The original quote in Isa. 26:11 can speak of physical death. Also, "the fury of fire" is a figure for a "blaze of intense anger." Zeph. 1:18 tells of the "fire of His jealousy."

The penalty in mind here is physical death not eternal death [Heb 10:28].

Even the verse which offers the best support for taking the warning as directed at unbelievers says those addressed have been "sanctified" [Heb 10:29].

"The Lord will judge **His people**" [Heb. 10:30].

By being sensitive to the arguments in Hebrews, one can take the warnings in Chapter 10 as addressed to Christians without implying a loss of salvation. Perhaps because Hebrews 10 gives such stern warnings, many who adhere to the doctrine of eternal security think the warning is for unbelievers. It might be better to think that God is furious at believers who forsake the Bible-believing church and associate with groups that insult the cross.

Assuming this warning pertains to saved people, an exposition results that still supports eternal security. The recipients have received the knowledge of the truth and are saved (v. 26). Should they now willfully sin by defecting from the church (vv. 25-26) and returning to associations with Judaism, they must not think animal sacrifices will continue to cover their sins and give fellowship with God (v. 26, see v. 18 which defines the cessation of sacrifice). Believers' sins are already forgiven before God in His capacity as Judge (justification by faith). However, believers also need daily forgiveness from God in His role as Father. The Christian readers of Hebrews must not think they can drop out of the assembly and return to involvement with Judaism without guilt. Jewish Christians who will not assemble with believers but instead return to affiliation with Judaism will incite a blaze of fury from God (v. 27). Those who set aside the Old Covenant deserved to die. Believers who set aside the practice of the New Covenant are more worthy of an even more horrible or painful death (or lingering death) than stoning. Though a genuine believer could not believe the theology expressed in v. 29, a believer who drops out of the church could promote these views by involvement with a false group (such as Judaism). If these Jewish believers withdraw from the church and return to

Judaism, they face God's wrath. [17] It will be "a certain, terrifying expectation of judgment" (v. 27). God
will exhibit fiery fury (v. 27).[18] Such defection and
cooperation with a system opposed to Christ deserves
a horrible physical death through God's chastisement, called vengeance in v. 30 (vv. 28-31).[19] The
warning passage itself can be understood as directed
to believers without concerning a loss of salvation.
The following section has been included to show
how this interpretation is consistent with, and even
supported by, the rest of Hebrews 10.

*An exposition of Hebrews 10:32-39:*

The close of Hebrews 10 also fits the above view
that the warning concerns believers who face God's
severe chastisement. Instead of forsaking the Christian assembly, Jewish believers must follow the
teachings in the rest of Hebrews 10. In v. 35 they
should not throw aside their boldness (confidence)
for the things of Christ. Continuance in commitment
to Christ by remaining in the assembly would lead to

---

[17] Please do not take this exposition of Hebrews 10 as bearing
Anti-Semitic feelings. As with the Apostle Paul, it is possible to
love Israel but disagree with its rejection of the Messiah (Rom.
9:1-5, 10:1).

[18] The "fury of fire" in v. 27 could just be a description of "fiery
wrath." Chastisement is like fire. The loss of rewards at the Judgment Seat is also like the burning away of worthless works (1
Cor. 3:15).

[19] Other cases of God's chastisement leading to physical death
include Acts 5:1-11; 1 Cor. 11:30; and 1 John 5:16.

"great reward" in eternity (v. 35). Endurance brings
the rewards that have been promised (v. 36). From an
eternal view persecution would only last "a very little
while" before Christ's return (v. 37). In the meantime
saved people should live their entire lives by faith (v.
38a). [20] (Hebrews 11 builds on this argument by giving numerous illustrations of justified people living
out their lives by faith. They did not allow persecution or peer-pressure to cause them to withdraw from
a life of faith.) God will be disgusted with the one
who shrinks from (forsakes the assembly v. 25) and
returns to participation in the synagogue (v. 38b).
The author speaks for himself in v. 39, but he also
assumes other Jewish believers will remain faithful
after they understand the full implication and dangers
of forsaking the church. We must not shrink from the
New Covenant and the church. That would lead to
the ruin (destruction) of this life either through wast-
ing this life by being out of God's will or through a

---

[20] The familiar quote in Heb. 10:38 is capable of more than one
interpretation in its original context in Habakkuk 2. "The just
shall live by faith" does mean justification is by faith as Paul
teaches (Rom. 1:17; Gal. 3:11). Yet, in Habakkuk 2 these words
also mean God expects those who are saved to face the coming
Babylonian invasion by having faith that God would keep His
promises. The author of Hebrews understands the phrase, "The
just shall live by faith" to mean, "saved people must live out their
entire lives in ongoing faith." All of Chapter 11 illustrates what
the author means. Jewish believers must not allow persecution or
pressures to hinder a life of faith as shown by the great Old Testament saints in Hebrews 11.

chastisement unto death.[21] Instead, those who live their lives by faith will preserve their soul. This could simply mean they face no danger of premature death.[22] However, it may be better to include the non-material aspects to man in the author's definition of *soul* in v. 39. Those who lead lives of faith, including not forsaking assembly with the saints, do preserve their psyche (Greek for soul) from much danger and pain.[23] The purposes for which a person's soul has been brought into this world can only be preserved by a life of faith. By lifelong faith a believer can pre-serve his soul (existence) from being a waste during its time on earth (1 Tim. 4:16 has a similar thought). The opposite would not be an eternal loss of the soul, but a ruin of God's plan for a soul being in this world. A life of faith gives the soul meaning as illus-trated by the lives of faith in Chapter 11. All the he-roes of faith preserved the purpose and the meaning for which God created their souls and placed them in this world. The Hebrew believers are expected to follow their example and not throw away the oppor-

---

[21] The word translated "destruction" in Heb. 10:39 is the same word translated "waste" in Mark 14:4.

[22] The Greek word *psyche* means "souls" but often refers to physical life in the New Testament, e.g. in Matt. 2:3-20 where Herod sought the Christ child's life (soul).

[23] The author's doctoral dissertation surveys evangelical rela-tives of those with schizophrenia. One principal factor which correlates with low scores of emotional adjustment is **withdraw-ing from church**. See Waterhouse, Steven. *Families of the Men-tally Ill,* D. Min. dissertation, Dallas Theological Seminary 1995.

tunities that God has for them in this life. The Book of Hebrews should not be used to deny eternal security. A modern application for preaching is that God is furious over believers forsaking Bible-believing churches in order to associate with groups that insult the Savior and the cross.

## Conclusion

Whether the author intends to warn unbelievers or believers, Heb. 10:26-31 must be interpreted in its original setting. The "willful sin" of v. 26 is "forsaking our own assembly" in v. 25. The phrase "there remains no more sacrifice for sins" (v. 26) means that the animal sacrifices of Judaism no longer cover sins after Christ's final and perfect sacrifice (v. 18). One view is that the author warns unbelievers (seekers who assemble with the church) not to reject Christ and return to Judaism. Those who commit this sin must not think the sacrifices of the temple will save them. Another more probable view is that the author warns believers about dropping out of the church and returning to involvement with the synagogue. These Hebrew Christians may not realize that such a move would give assistance in promoting views they do not accept. Also, God would respond to their disloyalty with fiery anger and chastisement even unto death.

If one still thinks Hebrews 10:26-31 disproves eternal security, he must be prepared to deal with the phrase "there remains no more sacrifice for sins" after "willful sin." If this warning concerns loss of sal-

vation, it is teaching salvation cannot be regained.
The author has personally counseled believers thinking of suicide over such unfortunate and needless
interpretations.

### *The fifth warning passage, Heb.12:25-29*

- See to it that you do not refuse Him who is
  speaking. For if those did not escape when
  they refused him who warned them on
  earth, much less shall we escape who turn
  away from Him who warns from heaven
  [Heb. 12:25].

The final warning passage of Hebrews does not con-
tain language as controversial as previous warnings.
Whether one thinks the warning applies to believers
or unbelievers, it is easy to see the words do not contradict eternal security.

### As addressed to unbelievers

If the author of Hebrews has unsaved readers in
mind, he is warning them not to refuse the invitation
to trust in Christ.

### As addressed to believers

If the author addresses believers, he is telling
Christians not to refuse obedience to God. Instead of
pulling away from the church (10:25) and returning
to involvement with Judaism, believers must "show
gratitude" and "offer to God an acceptable service
with reverence and awe" (v. 28). Those who do not

heed the warning will find that God can severely chastise them. The reference to "fire" is that of the chastisement of the believer (see 12:5-13).

## Conclusion to the warnings in Hebrews

Any student of the book of Hebrews struggles over the identity of the original readers. Are they un-believers mixed in with the Hebrew churches? Are they strictly Jewish Christians? Ones precise under-standing of the warning passages will be influenced by his conclusion as to the spiritual status of the readers. However, **both options can yield interpretations that do not involve warnings about a loss of salvation**. The author might be giving evangelistic warnings to unbelieving Hebrews. Maybe these Hebrews are seeking the truth and have assembled with the church to consider the claims of Christ. Of course, Jewish friends are urging them to return to the synagogue. If the recipients are unsaved, the author would be warning them to trust Christ to escape the fires of hell.

More likely the warnings of Hebrews are directed at believers. These Christians are being urged to drop out of the church and return to social ties with the synagogue. While they would still believe in Jesus, they face the danger of associating with those who oppose Christ. The author warns that a Hebrew be-liever who abandons the church will face God's fiery anger in chastisement during this life and loss of re-wards at the Judgment Seat of Christ. With either interpretation, one can consistently maintain eternal security.

### James 2:18-26

- But someone may well say, You have faith, and I have works; show me your faith without the works, and I will show you my faith by my works. You believe that God is one. You do well; the demons also believe, and shudder.... For just as the body without the spirit is dead, so also faith without works is dead [James 2:18-19, 26].

Additional study on James 2 is found in *Not By Bread Alone; An Outlined Guide to Bible Doctrine, pp. 143-44).* The key to understanding James 2 is that James defines faith as **only intellectual faith** in orthodox doctrine (e.g., v. 19). [24] That type of faith does not save. Genuine faith results in some level of good works at some time. If a person never has good

---

[24] Also, James seems to have a definition of "justification" that differs from Paul. Justification means, "to declare righteous." Paul writes of justification by God. Before God as Judge a person is justified by faith alone. However, James seems to refer to a declaration of righteousness by other people. How do others know whether a man or woman is saved? Other people declare a person righteous based on both faith and observable good works. Because of both faith and good works other people could declare that Abraham was righteous both in the sense of justified before God (saved) and righteous in living. Based on both faith and good works other people could call Abraham "the friend of God" (v. 23).

works, it reveals he has never placed trust in Christ, **not** that he has lost salvation.

It is virtually impossible to know how God would define a complete absence of good works; but James' warning urges an examination as to whether one has actually trusted Christ or just has intellectual faith in certain true theological facts. If a Christian worker notices a pattern of unrepentant sin in another's life, it may be proper to give him the gospel, assuming as a working hypothesis that such a person has not really trusted Christ. However, it would not be true to think the person has lost salvation. The situation in James would be that of one who has never been saved because his type of faith is only intellectual and not a personal trust in Christ as Savior.

### <u>James 5: 19-20</u>

- My brethren, if any among you strays from the truth, and one turns him back, let him know that he who turns a sinner from the error of this way will save his soul from death, and will cover a multitude of sins [James. 5:19-20].

The Greek word for soul (*psyche*) can refer to physical existence in this life. While most Bible students would take a phrase about a soul dying to mean spiritual death, the Bible often compares physical death to the loss of a soul. Sample references include the original language in Matt. 2:20; Acts 15:26 and 27:22. James 5:20 encourages turning back Christians from errors in doctrine and morals. Those who rescue straying believers can preserve a life from **physical death**. God's chastisement can lead to removal from this world (1 Cor. 11:30; 1 John 5:16). In addition, various sins naturally lead to physical death even without God directly causing death (immorality, suicide, alcoholism, crimes, etc). Proverbs constantly warns about the relationship between sin and physical death (2:18, 5:5, 14:12, 21:16).

The context in James 5 includes the possibility that some sickness comes because of sin. Thus, confession of faults may be a factor in God restoring health (5:15b-16). James closes his book with an extension of these ideas. One who leads a believer to repentance may very well be prolonging his physical life. The issue in James 5 is a possible loss of physical life but not a loss of eternal life.

## 2 Peter 1:10-11

• Therefore, brethren, be all the more diligent to make certain about His calling and choosing you; for as long as you practice these things, you will never stumble; for in this way the entrance into the eternal kingdom of our Lord and Savior Jesus Christ will be abundantly supplied to you [2 Pet. 1:10-11].

Peter's words are definitely addressed to Christians (v. 3). However, some Christians forget all the blessings that God has given. 2 Pet. 1:9 is a picture of senility. In comparison to old age, one who has been saved for many years can grow near-sighted to Christian blessings and responsibilities and can forget the blessings of his initial conversion to Christ.

In vv. 10-11 Peter warns against spiritual senility. Verse 10 uses a verb in the middle voice. It can be translated "make for yourselves your calling and election sure." As an objective fact, a believer's election is already certain. God will bring the believer to heaven. However, some Christians do not have the feeling of assurance over the security they possess. Diligence in the Christian life does not make a believer secure, but it can deepen inward assurance. One way to overcome nagging and needless doubts over salvation is to grow in the faith unto being like the Lord Jesus Christ in character. A life close to the Holy Spirit increases assurance of salvation (Rom. 8:16; 1 John 5:7, 10-11). 2 Pet. 1:10 urges believers to deepen their subjective assurance of salvation by diligence. By this a believer will not stumble into doubts and/or the practical dominion of sin. A believer will not stumble away from a life of fellowship with Christ.

2 Pet. 1:11 gives the blessing of such diligence. Peter is not offering an entrance into heaven by good works but rather an **abundant** entrance. Some believers will be saved but have little reward (they minimally enter God's Kingdom but will not enjoy an abundant entrance, 1 Cor. 3:15). Others who follow Peter's command will have an abundant entrance

into God's Kingdom. The alternatives in 2 Peter 1 are not salvation or the loss of salvation. The alternatives are assurance of salvation or doubts. They are mere *arrival* in heaven versus an *abundant entrance*.

## 2 Peter 2:20-22

* For if after they have escaped the defilement's of the world by the knowledge of the Lord and Savior Jesus Christ, they are again entangled in them and are overcome, the last state has become worse for them than the first. For it would be better for them not to have known the way of righteousness, than having known it, to turn away from the holy commandment delivered to them. It has happened to them according to the true proverb, "a dog returns to its own vomit, and a sow, after washing, returns to wallowing in the mire" [2 Peter 2:20-22].

Peter is definitely writing about unsaved people. The chapter begins with a reference to "false prophets" who "deny the Master" (v. 1). Other clues that these are unsaved occur throughout the entire argument. In v. 9 these are kept "for the Day of Judgment." Verse 12 mentions "destruction", and v. 14 says those under consideration are "accursed children." The description of being "without water" (v. 17) reminds us of lacking the water of life (John 4:14). The same verse says those under consideration have a reservation for black darkness (v. 17). Jude gives a parallel to Second Peter. In Jude 19 the false teachers are "devoid of the Spirit." Obviously, Peter's comment concerns unsaved people. He should be interpreted as discussing those who have never trusted in Christ (not believers who have lost salvation). These unsaved false prophets did experience a temporary escape from deep moral defilement through knowledge of the Lord Jesus. Knowledge here does not mean knowing Christ as Savior in the sense of trusting Him. They had factual knowledge about Christ and His teaching that led to moral improvement but not true regeneration through faith in Christ. Many unsaved people experience moral improvement by contact with Christian teaching. They know the Ten Commandments, the golden rule, the parable of the Good Samaritan, etc. Such knowledge alone is not saving faith but can improve morality.

However, Peter observed that those who experience ethical improvement without saving faith end in a worse situation should they return to their old sinful habits.[25] One who repudiates knowledge of God's holy commandments without ever trusting in Christ is worse off in at least three respects. First, he will probably be harder to reach with the gospel in subsequent encounters. A rejection of the gospel often causes hardening to future invitations to trust in Je-

---

[25] The same truth can be drawn by application from the Lord's teaching in Matt. 12:43-45.

sus. Second, those who repudiate the ethical standards of Christianity often swing their moral pendulum to even worse defilement than before contact with Christian standards. A rejection of the gospel along with a rejection of commandments for holiness can lead to deeper rebellion and wickedness. Finally, those who reject Christ against great knowledge of the truth will receive greater eternal punishment. The Lord seems to teach this in Matt. 10:15, 11:20-24; Luke 10:12, 14; and Luke 12:47-48. Those who turn away in unbelief and sin despite much exposure to God's truth will experience worse eternal punishment than those lacking such opportunities.

## 1 John 5:16

• If anyone sees his brother committing a sin not leading to death, he shall ask and God will for him give life to those who commit sin not leading to death. There is a sin leading to death; I do not say that he should make request for this [1 John 5:16].

The subject in 1 John 5:16 is prayer for a brother in serious sin.

Only God knows the nature or degree of sin which might lead to a Christian's removal from this life, but God will sometimes take sinful Christians home. John's words might be better understood without the article a: "There is sin (i.e. unspecified sin) leading to death."

Sometimes God chastens a believer with swift physical death (as in Acts 5:1-11). The phrase "I do not say that he should make request for this" (i.e. this situation, swift death) is not a prohibition against prayer. Rather it is a special exemption from the command to pray for sinning brethren. One could paraphrase, "I do not mean you are responsible and accountable to pray for brethren who sin in secret and then die suddenly, but you are accountable to pray for (living) brethren in known and serious sin."

The death of a friend can bring irrational feelings of false guilt. John does not want anyone to suffer false guilt when a believer dies suddenly, apparently through God's chastisement, and hidden sins are re-vealed after the brother's death. Sensitive souls might think a friend's death has something to do with their failure to pray even if they had no knowledge of involvement in serious sin. In situations of the unex-pected death of a believer in secret sin, John wants his readers to know God would never hold them re-sponsible to pray for a brother when they did not even know about his sins. They should consider themselves exempt from the command in 1 John 5:16, to pray for brethren in sin.

In most cases a believer in serious sin does not die suddenly. Other Christians have time to show con-cern and to pray for their brother's repentance. Though the believer still lives, he literally risks his life by continuance in sin 1 Cor. 11:30; James 5:19-20). Perhaps God's patience will end. Other times sin leads to a premature death through a slow wasteful process (Prov. 10:27, 11:19, 13:14, 19:16, 21:16). In situations where an erring brother does not experience sudden death, other Christians aware of the evil are under John's command to pray. Obviously, in these cases it is not too late for repentance, though stubborn sin does endanger life. Since John's subject is the risk of losing physical life, 1 John 5:16 cannot be used as a warning over the loss of spiritual salvation.

## The Book of Life

In Rev. 3:1-6 the Lord Jesus addresses the church at Sardis. Many in this church are dead v.2, (unsaved). Other aspects to church life are about to die (e.g. remnants of true doctrine and ethics). A few are saved, clothed in Christ's righteousness (v. 4). In Rev. 3:5 the Lord Jesus promises that overcomers will not be erased from the book of life. The same author, the Apostle John, defines overcoming as possessing faith in Christ in 1 John 5:4 (note the past tense). Therefore, Rev. 3:5 is promising those who have faith will **not** be blotted from the book of life.

- He who overcomes shall thus be clothed in white garments; and I will not erase his name from the book of life, and I will confess his name before My Father, and before His angels [Rev. 3:5].

A verse which promises that believers will **not** be blotted out of the book of life does not make a good proof text that believers can lose eternal life.

The Old Testament contains additional references to a name being blotted out of the book of life. Moses asks that his name be blotted from the book of life in Ex. 32:32. The Psalmist prays that his persecutors be blotted out of the book of life in Psa. 69:28. One interpretation is that the Old Testament may be referring to a book of physical life. The Bible speaks of God's books in the plural (Dan. 7:10; Rev. 20:12). The Lamb's book of life is definitely a book of eternal life. However, it is possible that the book of life in the Old Testament is a book of physical life. If so, Moses is asking to die. The Psalmist is asking for death for those who persecute the Messiah (Psalm 69 is definitely Messianic).

A second approach maintains that the book of life in the Old Testament is a book of eternal life not physical life. However, Moses' request in Exodus 32 is viewed as an impossible demand. God obviously declined Moses' rash and impossible request. Moses' words would be similar to Paul's thoughts in Rom. 9:1-3. If it were possible, Paul would trade his own salvation for Israel's salvation. Psa. 69:28 can also be viewed as concerning a book of eternal life. Suppose every soul is originally recorded in the book of life as having a potential for salvation. However, at death God blots out the names of unbelievers but keeps His promise not to blot out the names of those with faith. If the book of life begins with everyone's name, then Psa. 69:28 could be a request that those who directly killed the Messiah be eternally condemned (see Psa. 69:21). These may have been hardened so that they had no further hope of ever believing. Thus, when they died without Christ their names would be blotted from the book of life.

There are many references in the Bible to God's books (Ex. 32:32-33, Psa. 56:8, 69:28; Dan. 7:10, 12:1; Mal. 3:16; Luke 10:20; Phil. 4:3; Heb. 12:23; Rev. 3:5, 13:8, 20:12-15). The author believes it is best to conceive of many kinds of records and to take each passage in its own context without trying to see them as referring to a single book. It ought to be apparent that references about names being blotted from God's books need pose no problem for eternal security. They either refer to loss of physical life or to an unbeliever at death being erased from all potential for eternal life. Regardless, believers are **not** blotted out of the Lamb's book of eternal life.

## Conclusion on Eternal Security

This study has been an honest effort to address common objections to the doctrine of eternal security of the believer. Support for eternal security rests on the most basic teachings of the Bible (justification by faith, predestination, sealing of the Spirit, etc.). These truths are not unclear. Objections to the believer's security are based on verses that can *also* be interpreted in ways compatible with the security of believers. One can be grateful that often those who deny eternal security at least believe that they are

under the authority of Scripture for doing do. They
have what they mistakenly believe to be proof-texts
against eternal security. These believers do not possess the same attitude as liberals who do not feel at
all bound by the teaching of Scripture. Believers who
deny eternal security based upon mistaken Bible interpretations at least honor the Scripture by their
submission. For this they can be respected. Nothing
in this booklet should be construed to mean Arminians are heretics outside the family of faith. However,
the doctrine of eternal security enables a servant of
God to teach and counsel others with truth and without fear. Assurance of salvation is foundational to an
accurate view of God and self. Only from the basis of
the believer's security can we experience God's full
blessing in the Christian life.